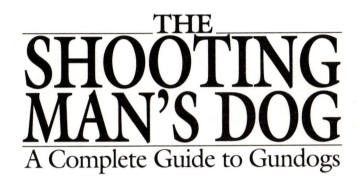

THE SHOOTING MAN'S DOG

A Complete Guide to Gundogs

THE
SHOOTING
MAN'S DOG

A Complete Guide to Gundogs

DAVID HUDSON

SWAN·HILL
PRESS

First published in the UK in 1995
by Swan Hill Press an imprint of Airlife Publishing Ltd

British Library Cataloguing in Publication Data
A catalogue record for this book
is available from the British Library

ISBN 1 85310 560 0

Typeset by Hewer Text Composition Services, Edinburgh
Printed in Great Britain by Butler & Tanner Ltd., Frome and London

Swan Hill Press
an imprint of Airlife Publishing Ltd
101 Longden Road, Shrewsbury SY3 9EB

Contents

Foreword

Shooting has been an abiding interest in my life from the time I was first able to hold a gun, and considered old enough to do so by my parents. Although there were always dogs of some kind or other about the house my interest in gundogs was somewhat late in developing, and initially I saw the dog only as a means to an end: something to find game and to fetch it after it was shot, but only a bit player in the course of the day's sport.

Now I find my attitude has turned full circle, and my interest lies with the dogs and the dog work. Shooting – although I still enjoy using a gun – is much less important, and I am quite willing to work a dog and let others shoot if there are others so inclined.

There is no better sight, for me, than a good gundog doing its job and doing it well, whether that job is quartering a moor for grouse, bashing through a thicket in search of pheasants or simply sitting quiet and alert beside a peg at a driven shoot. The satisfaction gained when your dog does a particularly clever piece of work is at least the equal of that felt when dropping a high, curling pheasant, or taking a right and left from a pack of twisting, contour-hugging grouse. Equally, the frustration when months of patient training are forgotten as the dog takes off into the distance in pursuit of a hare is more painful, and more abiding, than any amount of missed birds, however easy. At least, it is for me.

If I have managed to convey some of that satisfaction and frustration in the following chapters then I hope that I will have given an insight into what the shooting man's gundog means to me.

The Shooting Man's Dog

Depending on the strictness of your definition, there are something like sixty generally recognised breeds of gundog in the world today. Of the sixty breeds you can probably find around twenty-five resident in Britain, albeit in some cases in very small numbers. Some have been established here for centuries; indeed, many of our present 'gundogs' were being developed long before the introduction of villainous salpetre into the sporting field, while others have crossed the Channel only in the past few years. I have little doubt that the twenty-five resident breeds will soon become thirty, then forty, and perhaps eventually even sixty. The desire to own something better beats strongly in many a dog owner, and all too often 'better' is equated directly with 'different'. If you happen to own the only Gammel Dansk Honsehund in Britain, then by definition you own the best Gammel Dansk Honsehund in Britain. (You also, by definition, own the worst Gammel Dansk Honeshund in Britain, but I suspect that you are unlikely to view your situation in that particular light.)

But let us begin at the beginning. You want a shooting dog. You are going to choose your dog from among the twenty-five or so breeds available to you without making a sea crossing; at least, that is the assumption I intend to make. If you are absolutely determined to become the first owner of some exotic foreign breed then do so with my blessing, but don't look to me for advice. You are reading the wrong book.

We are concerned here, you and I, with dogs for the shooting man. Note particularly that I do not say 'with gundogs', though in truth it is only with gundogs that I intend to fill the next several chapters. I have shot grouse which were flushed (and retrieved) by a Border Terrier, worked in a beating line beside a Border Collie and even, many years ago, shot rabbits over a Miniature Poodle. No doubt someone, somewhere, at some time or other will have used practically every known breed, or combination of breeds, of dog to do the work of a gundog. Indeed, there is a well documented case of a pig being trained to point game for the gun, but I shall resist the temptation to include Large Whites, Saddlebacks and Tamworths among my list of companions for the shooting man, just as I shall exclude terriers, collies, poodles and all the other occasional 'gundogs'. They may be better than adequate; an individual may well be better than most gundogs proper, but they are beyond my terms of reference. Let us define those terms as 'gundogs for the shooting man'. (For the politically correct, yes, I know I should say 'or woman', just as no doubt you would have me say 'gundogs or gunbitches'. If it bothers you, then please be assured that throughout this book 'man' includes 'woman', and 'dog' includes 'bitch'. Except when it doesn't.)

So why not just say 'gundogs' and have done with the matter? Simply because I do not wish to set sail under a false flag. Of the tens of thousands of gundog puppies bred in Britain every year only a minority – and quite a small minority at that – are ever destined to march towards the sound of gunfire. Many, probably most, are destined to become family pets. Quite a lot will spend their 'working' life in a show ring; some will be trained as guide dogs and a few will spend their days hunting for explosives or drugs. All perfectly normal and more or less useful alternative uses of the gundog breeds, but beyond my remit. For my part, I am concerned with gundogs used for their proper purpose: as almost indispensable adjuncts to the man who shoots for sport. I could perhaps have chosen 'The Shooting Man's Gundog' for my title, but it smacks of tautology, and as such is best not littered across the dust cover in three-inch-high capitals.

Now it is a fact that, despite the twenty-five or so breeds which are available here, the vast majority of working gundogs are either Labradors or English Springer Spaniels. You will find them far out beyond the tide-line, huddled in a muddy gutter waiting for the geese to flight or high up on a Scottish mountain-top, hunting for ptarmigan among the rocks and scree. They sit at a peg on a September stubble as a covey of partridge bursts over the hedgerow; crouch beside their owner in a netting hide waiting for pigeon to flight to laid barley; or shiver outside a pheasant covert on a freezing January morning. They flush game over the guns from the beating line or wait far back beyond the guns to mark and recover wounded birds. The rough shooter relies on them to hunt out his quarry, be it rabbits from a bramble patch, pheasants from an osier bed or perhaps grouse from the August heather. Wherever a sportsman raises a gun to a live quarry, there you will find the Labrador and the English Springer Spaniel, hunting and questing, marking and retrieving, finding live game to shoot and bringing dead or wounded game to the gamebag. In the face of such versatility need the shooting man look any further? Should we perhaps be considering the Shooting Man's Labrador or English Springer, and ignoring the other twenty-three or so less numerous contenders?

Clearly not. If any one of the gundog breeds truly enjoyed total super-iority over all others, then sooner or later all those others would disappear, as working dogs at any rate, and that is not happening, and is never likely to happen. Coldly logical analysis might point the shooting man unerringly in the direction of a particular breed, but he would be a dull man indeed who acted only as such logical analysis dictated. Personal choice and fancy must also play their part, as must other influences: if, for example, the shooting dog is also to be a family pet then the family may require some input when choice of breed is to be finalised.

There is no such thing as the perfect, all-round gundog. Shooting itself embraces such variety, from foot-slogging for miles in the hope of an occasional shot at a distant grouse to being chauffeur-driven from peg to peg, there to shoot double guns at an endless stream of driven pheasants; from freezing in a muddy gutter under the light of a January moon to sweating in a bale hide while pigeon pour in to your decoys among the barley. Will your quarry be driven to you by a line of beaters, flushed from under your feet by a questing spaniel, found and pointed by a setter, quartering a couple of hundred yards out of gunshot, or perhaps hunted out of its burrow by a polecat ferret? Do you want your gundog to hunt for live game so that it can be shot or to find dead and wounded game after it has been shot? Perhaps you want a dog that will do all of the things above, or just one that will specialise in one or two things only. There are twenty-five breeds here already, awaiting your choice, and a further thirty or so available across the sea if there is nothing 'at home' that takes your fancy.

Before we begin to consider which breed to choose perhaps we should take a look at where these three score or so variations originated. The domestic dog, in all its many variations, has been selectively bred by man, starting, presumably, with the wolf. That your basic wolf can be transformed into such diverse forms as a chihuahua and a St Bernard, an elkhound and a corgi, says a great deal about the stubborn persistence of mankind, and not a little about our tendency to devote whole lifetimes to projects that potentially are as much use as mudflaps on a tortoise. Nevertheless, we have reached our current point in history with several hundred more or less useful variations on the theme of dog, of which, as we now know, some sixty or so can be grouped together under the general heading of 'gundogs'.

Consider this though: there were 'gundogs' some centuries before there were guns. They were not then called gundogs of course, but some, particularly the spaniel breeds, were already recognisable as the gundogs of today hundreds, and possibly thousands of years ago. One Dr Caius mentioned 'Spaniells' in his *Historie of Englishe Dogges* at the end of the sixteenth century, dividing the breed among those that 'sprung' game for greyhounds or hawks and those which 'set' game so that it could be netted. There are earlier references, right back to Roman times and even earlier, though there seems to be general agreement that the term 'spaniel' originated as a description of dogs which were imported from Spain.

These hunting dogs, which were to adapt and evolve into the gundogs of today, were used in a number of different ways in the pursuit of game. They would locate game by scent and then flush it out to be pursued on foot by hounds, or in the air by hawks and falcons. They would help their masters to drive birds into nets hung across their flight path, or they would 'set' game as it lay hidden in cover so that nets might be drawn over the quarry. In this they closely mirror the work that is done by our modern gundogs: pointing, flushing and driving game, for hawk or falcon in some cases, but usually for the sport of a man or men with guns. Gundogs they may be now, but the huntsman of centuries past would still see much that he would recognise among the dogs of today. I suspect the guns might come as a surprise though, as would the ways in which the countryside has changed.

The breeds may be ancient, but their sub-division and classification is relatively recent. The development of the dog has been going on for thousands of years, and the huge diversity of types which we see today is the natural legacy of those thousands of years of cross-breeding and experimentation. It is easy to see the relationship between spaniels and setters, or between Alsatians and Belgian Shepherds, and it can be quite difficult to distinguish between, say, Norfolk terriers and Norwich terriers, but it takes a little more imagination to see the common ancestors of a Lhasa Apso and a Pyrenean mountain dog. Nevertheless, the relationship is there, and somewhere in the distant past their genes must be the same.

The formation of the Kennel Club, and similar organisations, has largely arrested the development at a point somewhere towards the end of the last century. In the early eighteen hundreds spaniels were designated as Cockers or Springers according to their weight: between fourteen and twenty-eight pounds the dog was a Cocker, over twenty-eight pounds made it a Springer. Now of course a dog must have a pedigree attesting to the breeding of its ancestors before it will be considered as a pure-bred specimen, and unless it has such a pedigree to vouch for the purity of its breeding it will not be allowed to compete in dog shows or field trials, and neither will any of its offspring. Whether you approve of this system, as one that will help to keep the lines of our various breeds pure, or frown on it as a restrictive practice that positively discourages further development of the dog as a working animal, is largely irrelevant. If you think that you might someday want to enter your dog in a field trial or, God forbid, a dog show, then you had better make sure that your new pup is Kennel Club registered; 'cos if he ain't, then you won't be allowed to. Even if you have no intention of competing either in the field or the ring you would still be well advised to buy a Kennel Club registered dog. You might want to breed from him or her someday, and registration will add enormously to the saleability of the pups.

But let us return to basics for a moment. Why do you need a gundog at all? What can a gundog do in the shooting field that you cannot do for yourself? Agreed it can almost certainly run further and faster than you can, tolerate extremes of cold and wet that would have most humans in the terminal stages of hypothermia, and bustle its way through cover that would reduce your thorn-proof Barbour jacket to ribbons, but these are only relative advantages. Gundogs – indeed, all dogs, but gundogs in particular – have one ability that sets them so far ahead of us humans that we find it hard to imagine just how talented they are in this direction. The gundog has a nose.

By 'a nose' I am, of course, referring to a dog's ability to detect and distinguish scent, not to a physical organ through which it breathes. The nose is the main reason, indeed almost the only reason, for the development of gundogs. The nose is pre-eminent; all the rest has just been developed as a means of carrying the nose around to where it is needed. Gundogs work with scent. Yes, I know they have eyes and ears as well, and both play a part in their work, but they offer little advantage to the dog compared with our own eyes and ears. We can certainly see better than dogs, and though we may hear a different range of sounds our ears are probably just as useful. Our noses though are light years behind a canine nose in sensitivity.

The sense of smell is as important to a dog as its sight or hearing; it may even be more important. Whether your dog is used as a retriever, collecting shot game or as a hunter finding live game so that you may shoot it, it will be locating that game with its nose. Not with its eyes, not with its ears, but with its nose. Gundogs work with scent. I say it again with no apology for repetition, for it is this ability to locate game by scent, and scent alone, that is the whole reason for having a gundog. Take away that sense of smell and the gundog, as we know it, is useful as nothing more than a pet or a show dog.

Yes, I know it doesn't take a good nose to retrieve a pheasant which is lying dead on an open stubble field, but it doesn't take a dog to do that either. You could do it yourself. It doesn't take a good nose to chase a winged bird across the fields – as long as it stays in sight. As soon as it reaches the cover of the woods though, and ducks out of sight, you will need something other than sharp vision to continue the pursuit. You may be able to track a wounded bird through brambles and bracken by scent alone, but I certainly cannot. Neither can I find a grouse that is crouching fifty yards away totally invisible under a heather bank simply by winding its body odour, or track that same bird through five hundred yards of twisting peat hags by the scent left by its feet on the ground. I can't because I don't have the necessary equipment. A gundog does, and it can.

The nose is what matters; the nose is what distinguishes the gundog from its human master; the nose is the whole reason for those thousands of years of selective breeding and development. Take one nose and hang it on the front of a body which has been 'designed' to carry that nose in the manner which your chosen type of work requires. You want to find scarce grouse or partridge across wide open acres of field or moor? Then choose long legs and a light body which can be propelled for mile after mile, quickly and effortlessly. Perhaps you want that nose to bustle about in the undergrowth, pushing pheasants and rabbits out from brambles and thorn bushes? Then you need a short, stocky body with a thick, protective coat to turn away at least some of the prickles and thorns. The physical characteristics are needed to help the dog do its work to the best advantage, but they are needed because they are the best way to get that nose to where it is needed, across the particular type of terrain over which the dog is working.

Obviously gundogs will need all their senses when they are working in the field. Keen eyesight is needed to mark down fallen birds and to spot a wounded goose floating out with the tide; sharp ears can help to locate game which is rustling in the undergrowth or to alert the dog to the whistle of wings when duck are approaching the flight pond in the twilight. We use whistles and our voices to control our dogs when they are working, and hand signals to guide them on to birds which they may not have marked down. Nevertheless, a deaf or a blind gundog could still be useful under some circumstances, but a gundog with no 'nose' would be nothing but a passenger.

But do we really need so many different variations on the basic gundog theme? A lightly built, long-legged, fast running model to quarter the wide open spaces, a thick-coated, stocky, short-legged bustler to hunt in thick cover, and a heavier, stronger dog for retrieving large numbers of heavy game, probably with a warm, water-resistant coat and a good layer of insulating fat for retrieving from a wintery tide would seem to cover most eventualities. Three types only; yet in practice we have ten times that number working in Britain, and double that worldwide. Unnecessary repetition, or subtle variations which are genuinely needed to fill gaps in the market? The natural result of parallel development in various countries where slight differences in the work required led to divergence in the development of broadly similar breeds, or changes made for change's sake to satisfy the whims of fashion?

In fact the current diversity of gundog breeds owes something to all of the above. Take those breeds which are generally considered as 'British' pointing dogs. There is the Pointer, the English Setter, Irish Setter and Gordon Setter, plus the Irish Red and White Setter which you may or may not consider as a separate breed from its red cousins. And you may like to split the English Setter into Laverack and Llewellin types as well, giving us four, five or even six 'native' pointing breeds according to where you want to draw the line. Is there any practical justification for such variety?

There is an obvious difference between the Pointer with its thin, short coat and the longer-coated Setters. On hot, sunny days the setters can find the going tough, particularly if they are working on dry farmland or moorland. Conversely, many pointers hate the wet, and can be reduced to shivering wrecks if they are asked to work on a rainy winter's day. We have then a clear justification for developing two types of pointing dog: one to work in the heat of summer, and another for the depths of winter. Of course, as any bird-dog enthusiast will tell you, all the setter breeds are expected to work in July and August as well as later in the year, just as pointers are not confined to barracks as soon as the leaves begin to assume their autumn hues.

So there is some justification for the difference between pointers and setters. What then is the reason for our forebears developing four or five different types of setter? There are differences in temperament between the fun-loving Irish Setter, the sensitive English Setter and the phlegmatic Gordon Setter, but these are generalisations. There are serious-minded Irish Setters, just as there are Gordons which love to frolic and English Setters with hides as thick as a rhino. Since there are certainly common ancestors for all the setter breeds must we look solely at the whims of fashion for the real reason for variety among the setters?

Perhaps 'fashion' is the wrong term, it having derogatory undertones to those of us who earn our living outside the fashion industry. 'Personal choice' might be a better phrase. Indeed, there are certain gundog breeds which appear to have been developed solely on the personal whim of a single individual – the Gordon Setter being a case in point. The breed was developed by the Duke of Gordon at Gordon Castle, Fochabers, somewhere around the beginning of the nineteenth century. They obviously share common ancestry with the other setters, and such records as are available confirm this. Why then did the Duke's dogs tend to be primarily black and tan, when the other setter breeds are primarily red or white? Obviously because the Duke wanted things that way. He preferred his pointing dogs to be primarily black, and by judicious breeding he was able to produce the line that now perpetuates his name – incidentally, long after the title has become extinct.

But why black? The enthusiasts of English Setters, Red and White Setters, and Pointers as well will all tell you that their breeds enjoy an advantage over Gordons and Irish Setters in that their predominantly white coats help to make them show up better on the hill. As an enthusiast and owner of both Irish Setters and Pointers, and thus someone with a foot in both camps, I have to agree – up to a point. The white markings certainly do help when a dog has pointed three hundred yards away on what the Irish describe as a 'soft' day. If you don't agree with me that this is a significant advantage, then you have never worked an Irish Setter over rough ground on a wet day, and spent an anxious twenty minutes or so trying to find him, knowing (hoping?) that he 'must be' on point somewhere, just out of sight. Dark colours are a definite disadvantage on such occasions. Now I assume that the Duke must have experienced his fair share of wet days a couple of hundred years ago, though it was probably one of the keepering staff who scuttled about the hill in mounting panic when a dog went missing. The advantage of a light-coloured dog must have been self-evident then, and no doubt was well aired, since gundogs were a far more important item then than they are generally considered now. And yet, the Duke spent a great deal of time in developing a strain of predominantly black pointing dogs. Whim of fashion or personal choice? It really doesn't matter. What is important, though, is the understanding that there were and are other reasons than simply pure efficiency in the shooting field that have dictated the development of gundogs over the past few hundred years.

There have perhaps been parallel developments. On the one side there was the gradual division into setting, flushing and retrieving functions, with the different basic types of dog emerging, from the leggy, lightly built pointing breeds, through the stocky, cover-bashing flushing dogs to the sturdier, calmer retrievers. The development of the dog along these lines was primarily the development of its working ability. At the same time, though, breeders were selecting for size, for coat, for colour, for temperament, pace and conformation. There may have been good local reasons for some of these choices – a thick coat in colder and wetter areas; a particularly robust dog where the cover to be worked was unusually thick and thorny; a heavily built retriever to cope with the workload where particularly large bags were the norm – but mostly the different breeds have emerged as a direct result of someone's personal choice. It may be that they sincerely believed that they were producing a better gundog, or it may be that what was required was simply a different gundog. And no doubt for each of the breeds that are recognised by the Kennel Club today there must have been dozens of others that died in the development stages, or which became absorbed into other, more successful attempts at creating a 'new' breed of gundog.

Mr J. Walsh was the Editor of *The Field* in the middle of the last century and wrote under the pen-name of 'Stonehenge'. In his classic work *On the Dog*, written in 1859, he mentions the Norfolk Spaniel, the Russian Setter and the Welsh Setter in his chapter on 'Domesticated Dogs Finding Their Game by Scent, But Not Killing It, Being Chiefly Used in Aid of the Gun'. Of spaniels he writes: 'A great variety of these dogs exists throughout Great Britain and, until lately, they were divided into large spaniels (springers) and small (cockers). Nowadays, however, only four distinct varieties are acknowledged, viz – (a) the Clumber; (b) the Sussex; (c) the Norfolk; and (d) the modern cocker.' All of these were grouped under the general heading of 'Field Spaniels' which was then a generic name rather than a specific breed as it is now. Things have changed a little since then.

Shooting has changed, of course, as has the land over which we shoot. The partridge has declined and been replaced by the reared pheasant; the driven day replaced days spent walking-up with dogs. Different kinds of shooting sport have meant that our requirements of our dogs have changed, though they have not changed all that much. A pointing dog must still range widely, wind his quarry, and point staunchly until the guns are in position; a spaniel must thrust through cover to bustle up game for the gun. Within certain limits, their work has changed but a little. Why then, in just a century and a half, have the Norfolk Spaniel, the Welsh and Russian Setters disappeared, while the Springer Spaniel, apparently discounted as a separate type by Stonehenge, has returned to be the most popular of our modern spaniels?

Retrievers received little attention from Stonehenge. The 'St John's Newfoundland or Labrador Dog' was included in the chapter on 'Pastoral Dogs and Those Used for Draught', with a reference to the chapter on 'Crossed Breeds' wherein were the 'Curly-Coated' and the 'Wavy-Coated' retrievers, the former being a cross between the St John's Newfoundland and a Water Spaniel (generally Irish) while the latter was described as 'often pure St John's or Labrador, at other times he is more or less crossed with the setter'. I might also quote the opening of Stonehenge's section on the 'Wavy-Coated' Retriever. He begins: 'This fashionable breed is now considered a necessary adjunct to every shooter, even if he only attends a battue or a "drive" . . .' He was not the only writer to deal so dismissively with the Labrador, though now the most popular of all our shooting dogs is – the Labrador. Well, fashions do change, even when we are calling them personal preferences.

Buy a pure-bred puppy today and the chances are that he or she will come complete with Kennel Club registration and a pedigree form listing his parents and grandparents back for four or five generations. Should you wish you could certainly trace the breeding back for many, many more generations, through perhaps hundreds of different dogs and bitches. Many breeders can hold forth almost indefinitely on the subject, giving you chapter and verse on sires and dams long dead, and a fascinating subject it is – for those who are fascinated by it. Not everyone who is interested in gundogs will necessarily share this enthusiasm though. However, whatever breed your puppy happens to be, you may be certain of one thing: every dog and every bitch in that pedigree, for as many generations back as you may care to trace it, will be the same breed as the pup. Allegedly. There are the odd rumours of course, but let us accept the pedigree at face value for the moment. Of course they are all the same. You have just purchased a 'pure-bred' pup, therefore what could his ancestors be except pure-bred dogs of the same breed? Think back a moment to the situation as it was a hundred and fifty years ago.

Breeders then were still experimenting, still out-crossing and introducing new blood in order to 'improve' the strain of their gundogs. Hound blood was introduced: Foxhound blood into Pointer bloodlines, Basset Hound blood into Field Spaniels; Springers were distinguished from Cockers simply on the basis of their body weight. A single litter of spaniels could, quite legitimately, contain both Cockers and Springers: a dog could start its career as a Cocker and subsequently become a Springer subject only to fondness for the trough. To a considerable degree, dogs were categorised according to the way they looked and worked. If it looked like a Cocker and worked like a Cocker, then a Cocker it was. Nowadays, of course, a Cocker may look like a Springer and work like a Springer, but if the pedigree says Cocker, then a Cocker it is. You may make your own minds up about which system you prefer. Let us agree though that, whatever the pedigree may say, our modern, pure-bred gundogs are actually all a bit of a mixture from a hundred years back. All the spaniels share common ancestors; all the setters share common ancestors; and if you like to cast back a few more years no doubt you would find that there were common ancestors to both spaniels and setters. It may have been something of a hit and miss system but it was, after all, the system that produced the dogs we have today.

If you read enough books about gundogs – and I have read an awful lot, and hope to read more – you will eventually find that some author, somewhere, has championed one particular breed above all others. This dog, they will assure you, is the one dog that every shooting man should own. This dog, it appears, is simplicity itself to train, perfect as both a worker and a household pet, faithful, obedient and loyal and, above all, superior to all other breeds in the shooting field. Become the proud owner of one of these and you will never consider any other. Commendable loyalty no doubt, but logic dictates that, at most, only one of those authors can be right. There can only be one 'best' breed by definition. And in fact, there is no such thing as the 'best' breed of gundog. Too much depends on the work you are going to ask the dog to perform.

Even when you have identified the type of shooting that you are going to be doing there is still no quick and simple definition of the best dog for the work. You want a dog to work the open hill for grouse? Obviously you want a pointing dog. Which will be best, a Pointer or one of the setter breeds? My simple answer is that I cannot tell you. A good dog from any one of the pointing breeds will do the job for you, a poor one will not, or at best will do the job badly. One of the Hunt, Point and Retrieve breeds could also be the dog for you, though the same caveat must apply.

You would hardly use a spaniel or a retriever to find grouse out on the hill – or would you? Lots of people do, and every season lots of grouse are shot over spaniels or Labradors – and incidentally over all sorts of other dogs. You can, if the need arises, walk-up grouse without the benefit of any dogs at all, and if you are lucky, or there are lots of grouse, you might even shoot some. But I guarantee that you would have shot more with a dog to find them for you. And a decent spaniel or Labrador would definitely be better than no dog at all. However, a half-decent pointing dog would be far better than either.

Conversely, while you could certainly train your pointing dog as a non-slip retriever it would never match a Labrador at that aspect of gundog work. Nor will you ever persuade the normal run of pointers to relish burrowing about in a bramble thicket. Stand outside it and point, certainly; but if you want a dog to face thorns and prickles then a spaniel is going to have the edge on a thin-coated pointer every time. Well, let us say almost every time, because there are exceptions to every rule.

You may have a spaniel that will quarter heather with all the pace and drive of a field trialling setter, point its bird and hold the point indefinitely, and run all day without a break. You may have a pointer that will sit patiently by your side at a driven shoot, hunt assiduously for a lost bird, and perhaps even swim through the freezing waters of the estuary and retrieve a goose for you. It's the effect of all those common ancestors – by which I mean, of course, ancestors in common. No slight is intended.

It was long and dedicated work on the part of our forebears that developed the dog breeds which we have inherited today. They bred for nose and for pace, for build and for intelligence, for stamina and courage. They took the raw material that was available to them and by careful selection and judicious cross-breeding and out-crossing they managed to produce the dogs that they wanted. It must be said that there was also a great deal of extremely injudicious crossing and out-crossing, and no doubt an awful lot of dogs were produced that were anything but what was wanted. Nevertheless, they laid the foundations upon which all of today's gundogs, good, bad or indifferent, are built.

There have been many changes to the gundog breeds in the past century and a half, not all of them for the good. Several of the breeds dealt with by Stonehenge in his work of 1859 have disappeared. The English Water Spaniel is no more, at least not under that name, and we no longer separate Irish Water Spaniels into Southern Irish Water Spaniels and Northern Irish Water Spaniels, as was then the case. The 'Wavy-Coated' Retriever is better known as the Labrador, and is more common than Stonehenge could have possibly imagined when he disposed of all that he needed to say about the breed in just seven lines, albeit with a cross-reference to the St John's Newfoundland Dog.

To a great extent all the experimenting and developing has been halted by the rise to prominence of the Kennel Club, and their policy of only recognising for registration dogs which are 'pure' bred. This is largely a fallacy, since almost all of our dogs, if their ancestors are traced back far enough, will prove to harbour racial impurities in their background. Nevertheless, from now on, and for ever, we must only breed like with like if we are to remain in favour in the eyes of the Kennel Club. Any improvement to a breed must now be sourced from within the breed, and I am inclined to think that this is a good thing. The proper use of an out-cross may well provide a quick way to introduce some desirable trait, but it may also introduce other traits that are less desirable. And there is little doubt that in the past some breeders were all too quick to introduce 'foreign' blood in their search for improvement. Now, in theory at least, it can no longer happen, though it must be said that there is never any shortage of rumours. But let us return to the selection of the right gundog for the shooting which you intend to pursue.

I have said it before, and now I will say it again, and not for the last time. There is no such thing as *the* right gundog, no matter how narrow the variety of your shooting. Do you only ever shoot driven pheasants on large, well organised shoots with an ample number of pickers-up, and you want a retriever simply to complete your image and collect the occasional dead bird from around your peg? A retriever is what you require, but should it be a Labrador, a Flatcoat or a Golden Retriever? And if a Labrador is the choice is it to be yellow or black? Or chocolate? Do you do a little bit of everything, from the occasional driven day for fifty birds or so, through walking-up rabbits to evening flights on the foreshore? One of the spaniels perhaps? Or, indeed, one of the retrievers? And not forgetting all those HPR breeds: the German Pointers (Short-, Long-, Wire- and Coarse-haired), Hungarian Vizslas, Italian Spinones, Brittany Spaniels etc. Your choice is wider still, and that is the essence of the whole thing. It is your choice. Only you can decide what will be, or what you hope will be, the right dog for you. It may not be a single dog of course: you may need more than one dog; more than one breed even. Is one all-rounder better than two specialists? I can give you a pretty good argument to support either case.

We must also consider the variations that occur within each breed: two dogs with similar bloodlines, and even two dogs from the same litter, can have substantial differences when it comes to working ability. How much greater a variation can we expect from two which have no common ancestors, or not within the four or five generations which are detailed in their pedigree forms? Whatever I write about the different breeds in the chapters which follow it is important to remember that I will be writing in general terms, about those characteristics which are usually considered typical of the breed. If you require a pointing dog and you purchase a well-bred Irish Setter which subsequently refuses to point, then you will have my sympathy, but nothing further. There are atypical specimens of every breed, and it is entirely possible that had you selected a brother or sister from the same litter it would have pointed as staunchly as you could possibly desire.

You will simply have been unlucky. If however you require a pointing dog and have purchased a Cocker Spaniel in the hope that it can be induced to point, then I shall reserve any sympathy for a more deserving cause. Of course, you may find that your little spaniel is an outstanding pointing dog, in which case you have the sort of luck that would send me scuttling around to the nearest bookmakers with the housekeeping at the ready.

There are exceptions, and exceptional dogs from every breed. Perhaps it is some of those common ancestors surfacing many generations on. Perhaps it is down to exceptional ability on the part of the trainer or handler. Whatever is written about the characteristics and working ability of any breed there will always be exceptions – exceptionally bad dogs as well as exceptionally good ones – and if you find yourself with one of these then you must simply put it down to chance. Whether that chance is to be praised or cursed will depend on with which one you have been blessed.

But please remember, we can only consider the breeds according to their general characteristics. A particular breed may typically be calm, gentle, quiet, easily trained and an ideal house dog, but there can be no guarantee that the pup that you buy will not be an atypical specimen – hyperactive, bad-tempered, noisy, wild and destructive. You may just be unlucky. Of course, it may be that something in the way that you raised that puppy has made him into an anti-social outcast, in which case the fault is yours and not his or hers.

A guide to choosing, training and working gundogs can only be that, a guide. There are no absolutes, no hard and fast rules to follow, no promise that a particular course will guarantee success – though there are some methods of rearing and training that can be pretty much guaranteed to bring failure. Neither are success and failure quantifiable in terms that will apply to all: a professional trainer might consider the ability to compete at Open Stake level as a minimum standard commensurate with success, while there are plenty of practical gundog owners who are happy to tolerate almost any aberration provided the dog will hunt and retrieve. Most of us probably fall somewhere between the two limits – only you can say to which extreme you err.

In the end it matters little, provided that you are happy with your choice of dog, and with the way in which your chosen dog performs in the field. If this book can help you in making that choice, in understanding a little about why your dog behaves as he does, or if it simply provides some entertainment for a long winter's evening, then my own efforts will have been worthwhile.

Which Gundog?

At the beginning of this book I wrote that there are something like twenty-five breeds of gundog currently resident in Britain, and that the number of breeds will almost certainly increase over the next few years. Not only are there twenty-five different breeds but they are easily distinguished one from another, both in appearance and in style of work. How then to make a sensible and logical choice of one breed that will be right for you from among those twenty-five possible candidates?

Note that I do not say *the* one breed, since it is quite certain that there will be more than one breed which will fit your purpose, no matter how specialised, or indeed how catholic the variety of your shooting sport may be. Further than that, there will probably be two, three, perhaps four breeds which will be the main contenders to fit your particular specification, but close behind them will be another half dozen which, although less than ideal, will have the ability to perform your dogwork quite satisfactorily for all practical purposes. You may of course need more than one dog, and more than one breed of dog, particularly if you are fortunate enough to enjoy both low-ground and high-ground shooting, but you will doubtless still be looking for dogs that will work to that satisfactory standard of performance mentioned above.

Satisfactory performance will depend on several factors. You will obviously have an idea in mind of what you want your dog to do, and to what standard you want it to do it. If your intention is to win a Champion Stake then your minimum acceptable standards are going to far exceed those of the man who simply wants a dog for the occasional rough shooting foray and doesn't care how it behaves as long as it flushes the odd rabbit or pheasant. Most of us will probably have aspirations somewhere between the two extremes. Irrespective of this, the same three factors will decide whether the dog can meet your specification or not. They are, in chronological order, the breeding, the training and the handling of the dog. The right bloodlines should mean that 'your' dog has got the latent ability to carry out the work that you require of it: the right training teaches the dog to channel its natural instincts along the lines that you require, and the right handling should ensure that lessons learned in training are not forgotten or ignored when your dog takes to the shooting field.

Many, perhaps most, of the desirable qualities of a gundog are handed down from the sire and dam in the puppy's genes. Nose, drive, courage, stamina are all inherited, and if they are not there to begin with then no amount of training will produce them. At the same time it must be said that plenty of undesirable qualities can also come down from the parents. Some, like hip dysplasia, entropion and progressive retinal atrophy, are physical defects; others, such as lack of drive, a poor nose or a bad gait, are more to do with the dog's ability to perform in the field. There are other faults which may be either inherited or induced by poor training or handling – hard mouth is one that springs to mind, as is stickiness in pointing dogs and noisiness in retrievers. But these are considerations for the future. First you must decide which of those two-dozen-plus breeds is going to be your shooting companion for the next ten years or so.

The gundog breeds can be sub-divided into groups according to their normal type of work. The usual practice is to break the breeds down into four divisions – Retrievers, Spaniels, Pointers and Setters, and the Hunt, Point and Retrieve breeds. In theory you should be able to decide which you require: a retriever, a flushing dog, a pointing dog etc, and then make your pick from the appropriate group. In theory I suppose you can. In practice it is not quite so simple. Let us first take a look at the breeds which make up each group.

Retrievers

Labrador Retriever
Flatcoated Retriever
Golden Retriever
Chesapeake Bay Retriever
Curlycoated Retriever
Nova Scotia Duck Tolling Retriever

Spaniels

English Springer Spaniel
Welsh Springer Spaniel
Cocker Spaniel
American Cocker Spaniel
Clumber Spaniel
Field Spaniel
Sussex Spaniel
Irish Water Spaniel
Kooikerhondje

Pointers and Setters

Pointer (often wrongly called the English Pointer)
Irish Setter or Red Setter
Red and White Setter
English Setter
Gordon Setter

Hunt, Point and Retrieve Breeds

German Shorthaired Pointer
German Wirehaired Pointer
Hungarian Vizsla
Weimaraner
Brittany (formerly known as the Brittany Spaniel)
Italian Spinone
Large Munsterlander

The list may not be complete, or if it is complete at the moment at which I write it may well be incomplete by the time you are reading this. There are some thirty-five other recognised gundog breeds which are not on the list, and there is no doubt that more of them will continue to be introduced to Britain as potential owners look for something different as a pet, a show dog, or as a shooting dog. Nevertheless, it will do for the moment. Now, having made the list, allow me to draw your attention to some of the inconsistencies contained in it.

The first category is for 'Retrievers', and all the dogs contained therein will most certainly retrieve – but so will all the spaniels, all the Hunt, Point retrievers and, although it is not always considered a part of their duties, so will all the pointers and setters. So the ability to retrieve is not sufficient alone to distinguish the 'Retrievers' from the other three groups.

Neither can we take a negative view, and say that those breeds classed as 'Retrievers' are so grouped because they will not undertake the work that will be done by the other categories. All the retrievers can be, and are, used as flushing dogs, to shoot over directly or as beating dogs to drive game to standing guns. And some, notably the Flatcoats, may be quite efficient pointers; that is to say they will freeze at the body scent of game and hold steady until they are ordered in to flush the bird, rabbit or hare.

Then we have the Hunt, Point retrievers which are normally considered as in a separate category to the pointers and setters. In terms of the work they are required to do in a field trial this is a logical separation, since pointer and setter trials are normally held outside the shooting season, requiring the entrants only to show that they can find, point and flush on command, whereas at HPR Trials the game is shot and the dogs are required to retrieve as well. But when the first HPR breeds were introduced to Britain they competed in pointer and setter trials, and competed with some success until they broke away to establish their own trial circuit in 1962. The separation of pointers and setters from HPR dogs was not the result of the HPRs being unable to compete with the pointers and setters (as some pointer and setter enthusiasts will maintain), nor was it because the pointer and setter people did not like being beaten at their own game by the HPR breeds (which is the version of events preferred by certain HPR people). It was a logical development designed to allow the HPR dogs to demonstrate all aspects of their work, and led to the inclusion of a Champion Stake for the HPR breeds, first run in 1986. Incidentally, on the continent it is quite normal for the HPR breeds and the pointers and setters to complete against each other in field trials, including those stakes where game is shot and the dogs are expected to retrieve.

Consider the Irish Water Spaniel. I have grouped it with the other spaniels, but I might equally well have included it with the retrievers, since it is primarily a retriever rather than a flushing dog. Indeed, Irish Water Spaniels used to run in spaniel trials in England and in retriever trials in Ireland, though they are now considered as retrievers in both countries for trialling purposes.

Then there is the Brittany, which was called the Brittany Spaniel when it was first introduced to Britain, the name subsequently being shortened so that it would not be confused with the other spaniels. But what is the Brittany if it is not a spaniel? A spaniel which points certainly, and thus one which can work over a far wider front than the flushing spaniels, but it is still, unmistakably, a spaniel. Nevertheless, it competes in HPR trials and is conventionally grouped with the other HPR breeds, and I do not intend to flout convention. On this occasion.

We can trace much of this blending of abilities across the breeds back to those common ancestors we considered in Chapter One. It is hardly surprising that Flatcoats point when you consider their ancestry. The influence of the setters, both Irish and Gordon, can be seen in the head, the overall build, the coat and in the gait, so it is hardly surprising that setter influences should also be evident in the way the Flatcoat reacts to the presence of game. Not that pointing is confined to the Flatcoats; I have a Labrador which points quite staunchly, albeit only at a distance of a few feet, and many a spaniel will adopt a point momentarily prior to flushing its quarry.

Perhaps a better way of defining the boundaries between the four groups would be to say that each contains those breeds which share a common primary function. Thus those included in the Spaniel group are all primarily flushing dogs – with the exception of the Irish Water Spaniel – and those in the Retriever group are primarily retrievers. Let us forget for the moment that all the spaniels will retrieve and all the retrievers will hunt live game, and agree that, for the sake of convenience, they can remain in their groups for the purposes of this book.

Similarly, I intend to deal with the pointers and setters in a separate section from the HPR breeds, since that is the conventional wisdom. However, my personal feeling is that the division is false, and that it is wrong to split the breeds into two categories. They are all pointing dogs, and thus all dogs which can be allowed to search for game beyond the range of a gun. As to whether you require the dog to complete his work with a retrieve, or to allow another dog to do that part of the job for him, I leave the decision to you – though I will be returning to the question in some detail later. Let me say though that I think it would be interesting, and possibly instructive, to both camps if the HPR breeds were again allowed entry to pointer and setter stakes; with the corollary of course that pointers and setters would enjoy similar visiting rights to HPR competitions.

It is interesting that the designation of the newest of the groups is the Hunt, Point and Retrieve dogs, rather than simply Pointer Retrievers. Hunting may be included in order to establish that the dogs are required to search for live, unshot game as opposed to pure retrieving where only dead or wounded game should be picked, but in truth it is an unnecessary addition. All dogs hunt; the dog and his ancestors are hunting animals, and there is no question that the spaniels and the pointers and setters are hunters par excellence. Again though, I shall bow to convention, and HPRs they will remain.

Having broken our breeds down into four groups it is possible that the task of selecting a dog for work may be simplified. Note that I will go no further than 'possible', since the division into groups may be of little help to the sportsman who enjoys a wide variety of shooting, ranging perhaps from wildfowling below the high-water mark to waiting in a butt for driven grouse. Nor should we assume of course that a single dog will suffice for all situations. Certainly there are breeds which may be capable of doing almost everything that the sporting shot could ask of them, but there are no breeds that can do everything to the highest standards of gundog work. In the gundog world there are both specialists and all-rounders; and in general the specialists will beat the all-rounders hands down at the particular aspect of dogwork in which they specialise. Thus there is nothing to match one of the retrieving breeds when it comes to sitting patiently beside your peg while you rain pheasants down all around it; nothing to match a good spaniel at thrusting through thorn and bramble to flush pheasant or rabbit; nothing to match a pointer or setter at finding grouse on open moorland.

Remember that we are considering generalities here; there is no need to write and tell me that you know of a Vizsla that is the equal of any Pointer on the hill because I know of one too – but it is one individual, not the breed as a whole. I can introduce you to a Pointer that was as keen on retrieving as any Labrador or Golden Retriever, but in the same kennel I can show you another Pointer who refused even to acknowledge the presence of dead game. Again, these are individuals and not necessarily representative of the breed as a whole.

Gundog work – all gundog work – is about finding game. We may want our dog to find live game in order that it can be shot, dead game after it has been shot, or wounded game which has been shot but which is not yet dead. Three jobs only; and if you lump the second and third together under the general heading of retrieving, then you have cut them down to two. And yet there are all those different breeds. One reason, of course, is that there are an awful lot of different types of shooting. Which type, or types, you are involved in will largely determine from which breeds of gundog you should make your choice.

Consider the different types of shooting which we can enjoy. Driven shooting: standing at a predetermined point while your quarry is man-oeuvred to fly over you or run past you. Walking-up or dogging: where you go to the quarry and try to approach within gunshot. Flighting: where you try to position yourself along the natural flightline of your quarry. Decoy-ing: where you attempt to lure your quarry within range with some visual or audible imitation. Four divisions only which cover practically all the different methods of shooting – but what a host of sub-divisions there are within each category.

For three of the four divisions though, a retrieving dog is the main requirement. Driven shooting, assuming that you take part as a gun and not as a beater, decoying and flighting are all disciplines where the quarry comes to you, and your dog will have little involvement until after a shot has been fired. I know: in many cases the dog will have little involvement even then, but let us assume that at least some of your shots are successful. The dog then is required only after the main components of the task have been completed: the quarry has been brought into range, a successful shot has been fired, and now there is something to be retrieved. The dog is complementary to the main business at hand. Necessary certainly; without a dog you will probably not be able to recover all that you shoot, but he is not the main provider of the day's sport.

Contrast this with the final category: dogging and walking-up. Now the dog is no longer required to wait patiently until a bird is shot. Far from being a silent spectator to our skill with the gun, the dog is required to hunt out our quarry for us, to bolt it or flush in such a way that we can get a shot at it, and then to retrieve it when we shoot straight. You can get by at a driven shoot without a dog, though there will certainly be dogs present; you can decoy pigeons or flight duck with no canine assistance if you so choose, though your pick-up will certainly suffer; but you cannot hope to enjoy more than a tithe of the potential shooting if you take to the fields or the hill to walk up game without a dog to assist you.

The development of the specialist retriever has mainly taken place since the latter part of the last century, and is closely linked to the development of the breech loading shotgun which made continuous rapid fire a possibility. Shooting with a muzzle loader was necessarily a relatively leisurely occupation. Time was required to pour the powder charge, insert the wad, tip in the shot, add the overshot wad, tamp down the charge with a ramrod, prime the pan of a flintlock, or cap the nipple of a percussion gun and then cock the hammers ready to fire. Time was required, and time could be made available. For the sportsman shooting over pointing dogs, alone or with perhaps one other gun, it was quite simple to drop the dogs while the gun was being reloaded. The command 'Muzzles Up' – i.e. the gun being stood upright, butt down in order to carry out the loading procedure – survives today in that many trainers still use the command 'Hup' to order a dog to lie down. If you were one of a line of guns, then the whole line would halt until the fired guns had been recharged. Then, when everyone was ready you would proceed again. Which was fine for dogging or walking-up where swift reloading was not needed. Then, as breech loading guns became available, so the driven shoot, or *battue* as it was commonly called in those days, began to grow in popularity, and with the growing fashion for driving game grew the popularity of the specialist retrievers.

There was little point in being presented with a rapid succession of targets if your gun was empty, and you required half a minute to reload it. The sportsman needed to control the pace of his sport himself, only to proceed when he and his companions were ready. With the development of the breech loading shotgun, reloading became so rapid that it was no longer necessary to take a half-minute break between shots. The function of finding and flushing game could be separated from the shooting side of the sport, and the menials could be left to get the birds on the wing while the gentleman stood and waited for his quarry to come to him.

The concept of driving game was not immediately accepted by all Victorian sportsmen, and there was a long and lively discussion in the sporting press as to whether driven shooting was the pinnacle of shooting sport or a heinous betrayal of all sporting principles. Learned gentlemen argued persuasively that driving was either good or bad for the welfare of grouse, partridge and pheasant, and solemnly predicted triumph or disaster if the new fashion was allowed to proliferate. Eventually the pro-driving school won, and the *battue* became not only accepted, but the height of fashion for the Victorians.

Having been converted our ancestors then took the matter to excess.

Some – not all by any means, but many – shoots were run on the principle that the size of the bag was the prime determinant of the quality of the sport, and game was slaughtered in incredible numbers. No longer did the sportsman need to be capable of walking many miles across country to get to grips with his quarry; he could be conveyed from peg to peg, or butt to butt, in cushioned comfort, there to stand and shoot partridge, grouse or pheasant by the hundred or the thousand. There was no need for a dog to hunt out the birds for him; a team of beaters, flankers and stops would ensure that a steady stream of targets presented themselves above him. There was no need for powder horn, shot flask and ramrod; a loader could stuff cartridges into one of his pair of sidelock ejectors as fast as he could fire them from the other. There was no need for stamina, fitness or fieldcraft; the hard work could all be done by the keepers and beaters. Shooting had suddenly become as much a social event as a test of stamina and fieldcraft.

And the sportsman's requirements of his dog had been changed in the process. The fashionable shot no longer needed a dog to find live game for him since the live game was being induced to fly over his head by the hundred. What was required though was a dog to recover the dead and wounded game – a specialist retriever. The raw material was available in the form of the Newfoundland, the St John's Newfoundland, the Water Spaniel and the setters, and within relatively few years there were retrievers – Stonehenge separated them into curly-coated and wavy-coated varieties – to accompany their masters to the *battue*. They were not viewed with universal favour, as we shall see in a subsequent chapter.

There is no doubt though that in just a few years particular types of dogs were developed to meet the change in the requirements of the shooting field. They did not require the pointing dog's ability to gallop for miles over heather and hill, nor the spaniels' thrusting courage in the face of thorns and brambles. Rather, a calm temperament was wanted to sit patiently at a peg; a warm coat to prevent them freezing after swimming to retrieve on a winter morning; a strong build to enable them to carry the great numbers of birds that were shot; persistence to hunt out the line of a runner; good noses to distinguish wounded birds from among the mass of ground scent left by unshot game; and a handsome appearance to complement the appearance of their fashionable owners. In short, designer dogs, though I doubt that the Victorians ever thought of their handiwork in those terms.

It is clear that, in quite a short space of time, the Victorians were able to produce dogs to meet the changing requirements of the shooting field. In a matter of perhaps fifty years, by cross-breeding and line-breeding, the Labradors, Flatcoats, Curlycoats and Golden Retrievers were developed, accepted, and established in the shooting field. The dog was changed to meet man's requirements, and that is precisely how dogs have been developed over the past hundreds, and indeed thousands, of years. This amending of the basic dog model to meet our particular specification has been the making of all our gundog breeds. Unfortunately, it has also contributed in no small measure to the ruination of many, at least as working gundogs.

It is just as easy – in fact easier – to breed the work out of a dog as it is to breed it in. The time has come to consider the show dog.

Dog shows and field trials alike have been with us for about one hundred and thirty years; the first trial, for pointers and setters, was held in 1865, the first show in 1859. The Setter class at the show was won by a dog owned by the man who was judging the pointers. The Pointer class was won by a dog owned by the setter judge. It is entirely possible that both were worthy winners, and I shall suggest nothing to the contrary. You may think whatever you like.

However, prior to 1859, gundogs were dogs that were bred to work. After that date they began to be bred to be shown as well as to work. No problem there; but they also began to be bred to be shown instead of to work. Breeders began to select their stock on the basis of looks alone, without sufficient regard for the ability to perform the task for which the dog was originally bred. The result? I don't know how quickly it happened, but by 1907 Mr G. T. Teasdale-Buckell, in his book *The Complete Shot* was advising the purchasers of working gundogs to avoid those with show bench winners in their pedigrees. He said: '. . . of late years dogs have been bred for show without regard to their business in life; so that many exhibition pointers are only nominally of that breed, and instead of shows assisting pointer breeders they are so managed as to preclude competition by field trial dogs.' He develops the argument to suggest that only dogs which had won field trials or had been bred from field trial winning parents should be allowed to enter shows. It is an interesting argument, but one that presupposes that either field trial enthusiasts would want to enter their dogs on the show circuit, or that the show breeders have sufficient interest in gundog work to train their dogs to trial-winning standard.

Some, from both camps, undoubtedly would. There are some kennels which genuinely try to produce dogs which can win on the show bench, do a proper day's work for the gun, and/or compete in field trials. There are some, particularly in the HPR ranks, who are successful, even to the extent of producing Dual Champions – dogs which have earned both Show Champion and Field Trial Champion status. Among the longer established 'British' breeds, though, such dual purpose dogs are few and far between. The division between the workers and the show dogs has had a further ninety years to widen since Mr Teasdale-Buckell wrote his book, and in some breeds it has opened up to the extent that show-bred dogs are effectively useless as working gundogs.

The problem stems from the fact that, to many dogs owners, dog shows

Top left: Although it is not always considered part of their work, Pointers are quite capable of retrieving as Ferdy shows with this grouse.

Top right: A double handful of English Setters and Irish Setters awaiting their turn at a Pointer and Setter stake.

Above: Pointer and English Setter with professional gundog trainer Colin Organ and his wife Julie.

Top left: Golden Retriever with the darker shade of coat.

Top right: Pointer and Setter trials on a hot July day mean shirt-sleeve order for handlers and judges.

Above: The judges look on as a Pointer and an English Setter are cast off at a Pointer and Setter Puppy Stake.

Opposite: Pointer and an English Setter, eager to run on a hot summer day on the moors.

Top: English Setter hot but happy after a run on the grouse moors.

Above left: Three Gordon Setter puppies relaxing in a warm bed of clean straw.

Above right: English Setter, suddenly alert as something catches its attention.

Below: The Irish Setter has found grouse on the edge of a strip of burnt heather and waits motionless as the handler arrives.

Bottom: The ubiquitous Black Labrador which can be found on every type of shoot throughout the country.

Top: Red and White Irish Setter. Rarely seen a few years ago but becoming more popular; red and white was once the standard colour for setters in Ireland.

Above left: Black Labrador returning through the snow with a strong runner.

Above right: The Welsh Springer Spaniel is one of the older gundog breeds with a lineage traceable back for several hundred years.

Opposite: A snowy day in Scotland and the Golden Retriever looks to its owner for instructions after retrieving two pheasants.

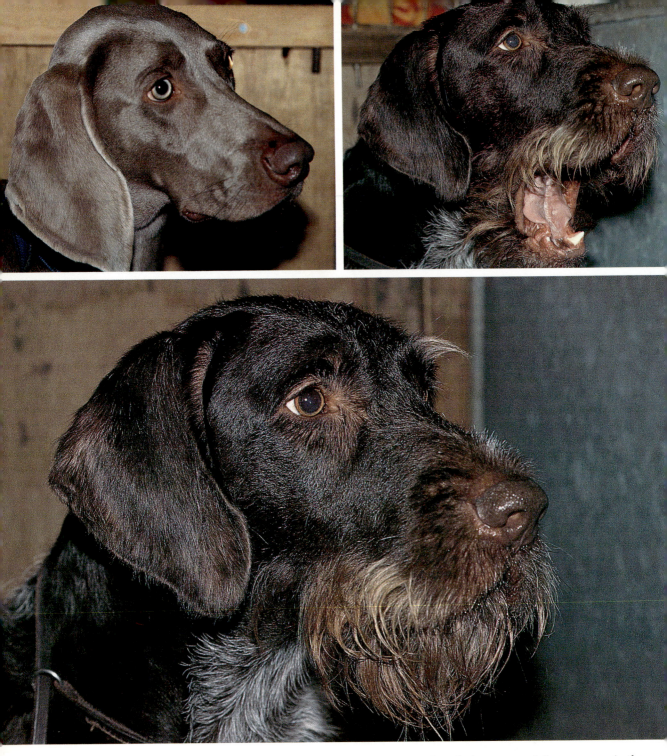

Top left: The Weimaraner is one of the more popular Hunt, Point Retrievers, though they are much less common in the shooting field than some other HPRs.

Top right: The German Wirehaired Pointer has good reason to look pleased. A regular worker on grouse and deer, he had just been awarded Best of Breed at a Championship Show.

Above: German Wirehaired Pointer. Not just a hairy GSP, but very much a breed in its own right, with its own way of working.

are the whole *raison d'être* for owning a dog. Dogs are born, bred and raised solely and specifically to compete in dog shows, where they will be judged solely on their appearance, and on the way they trot round a ring. There is no need for a show dog to exhibit any vestige of working ability. This is particularly sad where the gundog breeds are concerned. Some dogs – the toy breeds, for example – were bred specifically for their looks, and it matters little if show people continue to breed with looks as their main criterion when selecting bloodlines. Gundogs though were bred for their ability to perform in the field, and their size, conformation, coat and movement evolved in order to enhance and maximise that ability. Their physical characteristics were those best suited to get their job done in the most efficient manner. Contrast that with the show dog whose physical appearance is calculated, not to get a job done, but to catch the eye of a judge. And remember that, in many cases, the judge will know no more about the requirements of the shooting field than will the exhibitor.

The result is that we now have dogs winning in the show ring which would not be capable of doing the work for which their ancestors were developed: pointing dogs so heavily built that they could do no more than lumber about the hill with severe risk of hip and shoulder injuries; setters with coats so long that they would drag through the heather like a sea-anchor before becoming knotted into a mass of tangles; spaniels which have all but lost their drive and courage; retrievers from whom the retrieving instinct has been bred out. You can find any and all of them on the benches of your local dog show.

Let me try and strike a balance. If you happen to be a dog show enthusiast, and you want to show one of the gundog breeds, then good luck to you. The pleasure which many thousands of dog owners derive from shows has always managed to elude me, but there is no doubting that many people do derive a great deal of fun from shows. And I am quite willing to allow that many working gundogs have been allowed to deteriorate in their conformation until they are merely parodies of how a true specimen of their breed should appear. If dog shows could help to restore the correct conformation and structure to those breeds while retaining the essential working ability, then I would gladly concede that dog shows were a good thing for the gundog breeds. And I suppose they could – but the fact is, they don't.

If you want a working gundog, other than one from one of the HPR breeds, then be sure to avoid one that is tainted with show blood. You may find a show dog that will work – and by 'work' I mean work properly, not just stumble over the odd bird – but your chances will generally be immeasurably higher if you go to a working strain in the first place. It is a shame, and I wish it were not so, but that's the way it is. And if Mr Teasdale-Buckell was correct, that's the way it has been for the last hundred years. If you want a gundog to work, then you should if at all possible get a puppy which comes from established, working stock. And you need to be sure that 'working stock' means exactly that: the sire and dam should be working gundogs. This means gundogs that work, not pets or show dogs that 'would work if they were trained'. Every breeder can make that claim, and most gundog owners do, quite sincerely, believe that their dogs would make good workers if trained.

And, to be fair, they may well be right. Even in the showiest of show breeding the working genes are still lurking about somewhere. You might buy a pup from a long line of show champions and turn out to have an absolute cracker of a working dog. And then again, you might not. It is unfair to condemn all show-bred dogs out of hand as potential workers, but it is a fact that the man who wants a working gundog would be best advised to purchase a pup from working gundog stock. If you happen to know of a kennel that produces dogs which have the looks to win in the ring as well as the ability to perform their real purpose in life to a satisfactory standard, then don't let the taint of the show ring put you off buying one. Just beware of claims of working ability from those whose dogs do not themselves work.

But before you need worry about the breeding of your dog you must first decide on the breed, which brings us right back to where we started at the beginning of the chapter. Which breed? Your decision may be forced upon you by the nature of your shooting. If you live in the north of Scotland and shoot only over open moorland with a grouse density of one old pair per parish then you are going to require a pointing dog of some description. If you spend all your time below the high-water mark shooting wildfowl then I would suggest that you are looking for a retriever with a thick coat. If you are constantly invited to shoot driven pheasants by the hundred . . . but you know what you are going to shoot. Or perhaps you don't, and you want an all purpose gundog that will be acceptable everywhere from moor to shore. The choice is yours; all I can do is to try and present you with a fair summary of the alternatives. And that is what I will attempt in the following chapters.

Retrievers

Let us begin by going back a few years, to 1907 in fact, and let us consider the views of one writer on retrievers. He – Mr Teasdale-Buckell again, incidentally – said:

'People purchase and use retrievers for either one or more of several reasons:
1. Because they like a dog.
2. Because they like to collect more game than they shoot.
3. Because they do not like to leave wounded things to die in pain.
4. Because when they are out of the house they like to have something that they can order about.
5. Because the dead game that can be seen is easy for the dog to retrieve.
6. Because the wounded game that cannot be seen is difficult for men to pick up.
7. Because a handsome retriever gives a finish almost equivalent to neat spats to a shooter's turn-out.
8. Because it is much easier to gain credit for sportsmanship at a dog show than in the field and covert.
9. Because there is a demand for stud services at remunerative fees.'

Obviously they are not all applicable to the modern field sportsman. Very few shooters wear spats these days. As for the rest, let us just say that Mr Teasdale-Buckell obviously knew what he was writing about then, and he probably wouldn't want to change too much if he was writing today.

However, the chapter from which I have quoted began 'Retrievers are now by far the most popular gundogs in this country . . . ', and in that respect things have certainly not changed. Almost a century later retrievers are still far and away the most popular gundogs in the country. For the retrievers to have gained that popularity in the first place could be attributed to the whims of fashion; for them to have held that position for a hundred years must mean that there are sound reasons for the choice of a retriever as the shooting man's dog.

And, of course, there are. Labradors and Golden Retrievers are among the most popular of dogs – all dogs, not just gundogs. They invariably feature near or at the top of the Kennel Club's annual registration statistics. And let me repeat: these numbers apply to all dogs registered, the pets and the show dogs as well as the working gundogs, and is therefore a clue to the reason for the popularity of these breeds. They are in demand as pets because of their temperament, and they are popular in the show ring because of their appearance. The combination of working gundog with good-looking, easily handled, calm and equable family pet is in itself sufficient reason for their abundance.

Beyond that though, there is no doubt that for many, perhaps for the majority of shooting men, a retriever is exactly what their type of shooting requires. Driven game shooting, wildfowling, flighting and decoying are all basically 'retriever only' activities. Rough shooting and walking-up need a dog that can hunt and flush as well as retrieve, but the retrievers can tackle those aspects as well as fulfilling their primary function of retrieving. It is only when 'dogging' – shooting over one of the pointing breeds – that it is absolutely necessary to have a specialist on the team. In nine cases out of ten a good retriever can do everything that the shooting man will want of his gundog.

And, similarly, in nine cases out of ten 'retriever' means Labrador Retriever. The ubiquitous Labrador can be found over the length and breadth of the country, sitting at a peg beside a titled owner at the poshest of posh pheasant drives or crouching in a muddy gutter far out on the foreshore. There are Labs on the grouse moor and Labs on the rough shoot; Labs under the camouflage nets of pigeon hides and Labs beavering away in the beating line; Labs picking up, Labs dogging in poults around the shoot boundaries and Labs winning field trials and working tests and gundog scurries. The beggars are everywhere!

And yet, at the beginning of the century the Labrador took a back seat to the Flatcoats and Curlycoats. The popularity of the retrievers as a group had flowered with the fashion for driven game shooting, and a great deal of experimental breeding took place in the latter half of the nineteenth century. Stonehenge, writing in 1859, deals with the retrievers in his chapter entitled 'Crossed Breeds' under the headings of 'The Curly-Coated' and 'The Wavy-Coated'. The origins of the Labs come in the chapter on 'Pastoral Dogs and Those Used for Draught', being split under the sub-heading of 'The Newfoundland and Labrador Dog' into three categories: The True New-foundland, The Landseer Newfoundland, and The St John's or Labrador.

Fifty years later Mr Teasdale-Buckell divided the retrievers as follows: 'In England there are three sorts of retriever, and crosses between each, besides Labradors and spaniels. These three are the flat-coated variety, the curly-coated sort and the Norfolk retriever, with its open curl or wave of coat.'

Note that the Labrador was then, at least in one writer's view, considered slightly apart from 'the retrievers'. Indeed, it was afforded a short chapter of its own in the book, and not all of the author's remarks were complimentary. Compare this with the situation thirty-five years later. The authoress this time is Lorna, Countess Howe, writing in *Hounds and Dogs*, a Lonsdale Library publication of 1943. She writes: 'The Labrador unquestionably holds premier position of all breeds of working retrievers. It is amazing to see at private shoots the number of Labradors owned by shooting men and gamekeepers.'

Thus, in a relatively short time, the Labrador went from being an also-ran to the position of most popular gundog, a position which it still holds to this day. There is of course an element of self-regeneration in that popularity. If you are looking for a gundog pup, then the majority of working-bred pups on offer at any time are going to be Labradors. And having purchased your Labrador bitch and decided a few years later to take a litter from her you will be adding to the pool of working Labs. However, such self-regeneration can only be a partial reason for the continuing popularity of the breed; it cannot explain the reasons for the initial rise in popularity of the Lab at the expense of the Flatcoats, the Curlycoats and those Norfolk Retrievers with their 'open curl or wave of coat'. These breeds were once the pre-eminent retrieving breeds until the Labrador overtook them. It is an indication of the ability of the Labrador that it has never since slipped back in the shooting man's esteem.

Pre-eminent though the Labrador may be, it is far from being the only working retriever worthy of consideration. Golden Retrievers match the Labradors closely in terms of the number of dogs registered through the Kennel Club, though they are much less common in the shooting field. Flatcoats, at one time the most popular of the retrieving breeds, are still to be found working on shoots throughout the country, and plenty of kennels of working Flatcoats remain. Curlycoats and Chesapeake Bay Retrievers are certainly much less common, but it is possible to obtain dogs of either breed from proven working stock. You will certainly have to look harder than if you had decided to follow convention and invest in a Labrador, but all the breeds are still worked, and stock from all is available.

So, which one should you choose? Logic says that the answer should be a Labrador, since with the Labrador lies the widest possible choice and the most diverse gene pool. The accumulated wisdom of other shooting men would also tend to point in the Labrador's direction; can those thousands of working Labrador owners really all be wrong? You may elect to follow logic and conventional wisdom, and who am I to argue with that? However, just in case you might want to fly in the face of convention, we should perhaps consider all the retrieving breeds before making that final decision. Let us begin with the most common.

The Labrador

There are many references to Labradors in books written during the last century, but these are sometimes more a hindrance than help in tracing the origins of the modern Labrador. The Labrador certainly originated with dogs brought back from Newfoundland by fishermen. The larger New-foundland dogs can still be found today, though they are not used in the shooting field, nor were they then. A smaller variety, called the St John's Newfoundland or Labrador, is the direct ancestor of today's working Labs, but it is also probably deeply involved in the ancestry of the Flatcoated and Golden Retrievers as well.

What is less clear is how the dogs reached North America in the first place, though it is almost certain that they were originally taken there from Europe, possibly by predecessors of the same fishermen credited with their reintroduction. They were used by Grand Banks fishermen as boat dogs and thus developed their great affinity for water, and it was this love of water and instinct for retrieving that attracted the attention of British sportsmen when specimens of the breed were brought 'home' again. There is also some evidence to suggest that many of the 'imported' dogs sold by fishermen in the last century were in fact home-bred, the 'imported' label being added to boost the price which the pup would fetch. There was no Trade Descrip-tions Act in the middle of the nineteenth century.

No matter: the modern Labrador certainly descends directly from the St John's Newfoundland, though how direct that descent is will depend on which school of thought you elect to follow. One theory holds that the Labrador is mainly pure-bred from the St John's Newfoundland, though Stonehenge maintained that the St John's Newfoundland was 'more or less crossed with the setter or spaniel . . . ' and was then '. . . commonly known as "a retriever" . . . ' You may take your pick; the end result is the Labrador which we all know today and, unless you are a student of canine history, it probably won't bother you overly if you don't know exactly where its great-great-great-great-grandparents originated.

Whatever those origins, by the early years of the twentieth century the Labrador was firmly established as a breed. The first Lab to win a prize at a field trial was Munden Single who collected a Certificate of Merit at an International Gundog League trial in 1904; the first Labrador Field Trial Champion was made up in 1908 – a dog called Flapper, owned by a Major Portal. From then onwards Labradors were regularly among the awards and their numbers increased spectacularly. The Kennel Club have main-tained figures for the number of Labradors registered, and that number has increased from under three hundred in 1912 to over three thousand in 1952, and up to almost fourteen thousand by the seventies.

There is no doubting the Labrador's popularity as a pet, a show dog, and most importantly in the shooting field. The Labrador has an awful lot going for it when the shooting man comes to choose his dog:

1. There is never any problem in finding a Labrador puppy from proven working stock.

2. Since Labradors are so readily available there is no problem in finding a pup at a price to suit your pocket. Certainly, if you wish you can pay a great deal of money for a pup which may – and I stress, *may* – turn out to be a class apart from the general run of Labs, but there is no need to do so. Somewhere near you there will be a litter of Labradors for sale at a price which you will consider reasonable.

3. Should you want your Lab trained for you, you will have no difficulty in finding either a trained dog or an experienced dog trainer ready to convert your little treasure into a highly skilled and willing worker. In return for an appropriate consideration of course.

4. And if you prefer to do it yourself, Labs are generally very quick to learn, responsive, and easy to train. Generally.

5. You can arrive at any shoot, anywhere, accompanied by a Labrador without causing raised eyebrows and snide asides. Of course, depending on what happens after you arrive . . .

6. Labs mature early and may well be working in the field when some other breeds are still in basic training.

7. If your gundog has to double as house pet, kiddie's plaything, security guard, organic waste disposal device and occasional drinking companion, then a Lab will happily undertake the extra workload. Especially the waste disposal bit.

8. On the subject of house dogs, Labs have reasonably short coats that won't trail too much mud and muck into your house and car and don't require a great deal of grooming.

9. The most important bit. Labradors generally are damn good at their work, whether they are sitting patiently as non-slip retrievers or working their socks off in the beating line; freezing on the foreshore, picking-up way behind the line and dealing with all the runners and lightly pricked birds; beavering about walking-up, or crouching motionless in a decoyer's hide. Whatever you want done, short of bird-dog work, a Labrador will do it for you. And if you've got one from working stock and trained it right the chances are that it will do the job pretty much as good as anything else; maybe even better.

So there are nine good reasons to buy a Labrador. I could probably have sorted out a tenth with a little more thought, but I rather like the idea of following the precedent set by Mr Teasdale-Buckell. Reading them through I seem to have made a pretty good case for the Labs, good enough so that you may be wondering why we don't pack it in right here and start perusing the small ads for Labrador litters or trainers. We'll deal with that question when we start looking at the Flatcoats, Curlycoats, Goldens and Chesapeake Bay Retrievers, but for the moment let us concentrate on the undoubtedly talented Labrador.

Labs come in three choices of colour. Black, which is the colour of the majority of the working dogs; yellow, which is the colour of practically all the rest; and occasionally a sort of livery-brown shade which is known as chocolate. I have seen both good and bad workers of all three shades, and as far as I am aware there is no practical difference in ability between dogs of differing colours. Indeed, a single litter may contain puppies of more than one colour, so logically any inherited ability would be as strong in yellow dogs as in black dogs as in chocolate ones. If you have a preference as to colour then indulge it; it is unlikely to affect the latent ability of your dog, though you will certainly find it harder to locate a chocolate pup from working parents than to find a black or yellow one.

What about looks? Another quote from Stonehenge to start us off: 'Fancy dogs [show dogs] may be measured by any rule, however artificial, but a shooting dog should only be judged by the points which are relevant to his work.' Put more simply, it's how the dog works which counts, not how it looks. Up to a point. Show people breed for looks and looks alone, and have a tendency to exaggerate certain points. For example, Pekes are supposed to have snub noses, but not noses so snub that they can no longer breathe through them. The same type of thing happens with show gundogs. Irish Setters are supposed to have feathery coats, but not such feathery coats that they would never be able to run on a hill without getting knotted down in the heather. Show Labradors are big and handsome with the appropriate broad skulls and otter tails, but without necessarily being stuffed with working ability.

There are plenty of working Labradors about that measure up well to the breed specification. There are also quite a lot that do not. Undersized, snipey-headed, thin-tailed or short-legged, and possibly all of the above, some working Labs are not exactly a walking advertisement for the breed. Now I know you are about to look back at the last paragraph and remind me I have just written that it is how they work that is important, and not how they look, and you are quite right. Up to a point. To my mind, though, a Labrador which has become too small, too snipey, too short on the leg, has somehow lost the essential 'Labradorness' which it should have about it. I do like a dog which looks right as well as doing the job right. That said, if it came down to a choice between an undersized dog that worked and a big, handsome drone that didn't, then the worker would be the one that got the kennel space. I would however think twice before breeding from it. You may not feel the same way about the matter. However, if you do, then rest assured that it should not be too difficult to find a good-looking dog which also has its full complement of latent working ability. How well that latent ability is developed will depend on your ability as a trainer (or the ability of the trainer of your choice) and the amount of work that the dog is given once the training period is over.

Work for a Labrador can take many different forms. Perhaps the traditional picture of a Lab at work would show it sitting beside its owner at a peg, or in a butt, while pheasants, partridges or grouse were driven over. All eager attention, our Lab would be marking the fall of each bird ready to get out and retrieve at the end of the drive. Of course, depending on the temperament, our Lab might be curled up asleep oblivious to the rattle of musketry, or it might be plunging and leaping in wild excitement, maintaining station only due to the presence of a patent dog tether and six feet of half-inch hawser. Your typical Lab may combine eager alertness with patience and restraint, but there are more than a few at either end of the spectrum, the sleeping beauties as well as the madly eager types.

The man who shoots mainly or exclusively at driven shoots is likely to use his dog almost entirely as a retriever. At the opposite end of the spectrum there are plenty of Labradors that spend most of their working lives in the beating line, hunting and flushing live game and rarely being asked to do any actual retrieving. In between the two is the rough shooter's dog which is expected to hunt and flush live game for the gun and to retrieve dead and wounded birds after the shot. The more placid temperament would seem to be best suited to sitting patiently while master rains game down all around it, just as something a bit more lively is probably required if you want your dog to spend eight hours a day forcing its way through thick cover in search of rabbits and pheasants. That just leaves the question of what temperament to go for if, like me, you mix rough shooting, beating, some driven shooting, a few days picking up and a few evenings dogging-in pheasant poults – all in the course of one season.

Some Labradors can be so calm and placid that you feel like prodding them from time to time to see if they are still exhibiting any signs of life. Laid back may be good, but to my mind there is a limit, and when a dog no longer looks interested in its work then it is probably getting somewhere about that limiting point. We go shooting because we enjoy it, and the same should go for our dogs. The overweight, under-exercised archetypal 'fat Lab' is not just a figment of the cartoonist's imagination, they do exist. You probably know one yourself. There are, of course, plenty of owners who want a quiet and placid dog, and nothing is quieter and more placid than a Labrador – provided that it is one of the quiet and placid type. There are also quite a few around which have a rather different attitude to life.

Now, almost every shoot will have one. You know the dog I mean: the one which runs amok as soon as it manages to slip its head out of its collar, riots through the next three drives, chases every hare and rabbit on the place, picks up your shot birds from under the nose of your own dog, steals your sandwiches at lunchtime and plants muddy paw prints all over the cushions in your new Range Rover. Sometimes, I regret to say, this little monster will be a Labrador – one of the more active types of course.

It is debatable whether it is the breeding of the dog or the ability of the owner which is to blame. There are some owners who seem to be able to take the quietest most peaceful dog and convert it into a monster. There are also some Labs which seem to have the monster market pretty well sewn up all by themselves. The really serious trouble starts when one of those owners of the first part gets hold of one of the dogs of the second part to train. You know them? So do I, and so do the rest of us. However, unless you want a sleepwalker, or a hyperactive nutcase – and I appreciate that some owners do actually want their gundog to come from one extreme or the other – it is as well to bear the extremes in mind when selecting your Labrador pup. The temperament of the parents is a guide, and even as puppies there are usually a few tell-tale signs to point you to the way in which the pup is likely to develop. The ideal Lab should be alert and active, easy and willing to train, and quick to learn. The retrieving instinct is so strongly developed in the breed that most will start fetching you things from the moment they are strong enough to pick something up and carry it.

This can be a mixed blessing: you and your pup are unlikely to have the same values initially, and a series of eagerly fetched gifts of dead rats, dried cowpats and stinking old bones can easily begin to annoy – particularly if you are following the advice of the training manuals and never, ever scolding your pup for retrieving, whatever the object retrieved. Many Labs seem to be ill at ease unless they are parading around with something – anything – in their mouths, and you may well get tired of finding your slippers and shoes scattered all over the house. On the other hand, there is a certain satisfaction in having your slippers brought to you as you come in the door. Even though you may not be ready to put them on.

The painful and crippling hereditary defect hip dysplasia is not uncommon in Labradors, and you should be aware of the danger when selecting your puppy. Many breeders have their dogs checked by X-ray for signs of the defect, and may include the 'scoring' of the parents in their advertisement for puppies. The lower the score the better. It is not confined to Labradors of course.

The Golden Retriever

There is a story that all Golden Retrievers are descended from a troupe of Russian circus dogs which were purchased by Lord Tweedmouth and dispatched to his estate at Guisachan. It is an appealing story but probably not a true story. The truth, which can be extracted from the detailed, personal records which Lord Tweedmouth maintained, is more prosaic, today's Goldens beginning as a mixture of Tweed Water Spaniel, Bloodhound, Irish Setter, Flatcoat and Labrador.

Lord Tweedmouth undoubtedly managed to establish a breed of yellow-coloured retrievers, and it is from this foundation stock that the Golden Retrievers have descended. The breeding programme took place over the last third of the nineteenth century, so the Golden Retriever is a relatively recent arrival on the British gundog stage, though its ancestors have been around a lot longer. The breed was first recognised by the Kennel Club in 1913 as 'Yellow or Golden Retrievers', the 'Yellow' part of the name being dropped seven years later in 1920.

They are hugely popular both as pets and among dog show enthusiasts, and it must be said that being in demand as pet and show dogs is not a good thing as far as preserving and developing their working ability is concerned. Although the number of Goldens registered annually with the Kennel Club will match, and even exceed, the number of Labradors on occasion, they are nowhere near as common as the Labrador in the shooting field.

There are several possible reasons for this. The Golden Retriever is generally a slower dog to mature than its cousin the Labrador and may well still be in basic training when a Lab of the same age would have a season or more of experience in the line of fire. This alone is sufficient reason to steer many a potential owner away from the Golden and in the direction of the Labrador. Their coats are longer and finer than those of Labradors and need a lot more grooming, particularly after working in thick cover. Indeed, the coat of some show dogs has been encouraged to develop to the extent that it would be a positive handicap if the dogs were ever expected to work among thorns, brambles and briars.

The yellow or golden colour which was once typical of the Golden Retriever has been replaced in many dogs by an almost white coat, much favoured by the show fraternity, but not terribly practical for a working gundog. The sheer numbers being bred for show and pet homes also tend to muddy the waters when you are looking for a working pup. All too many advertisers of gundog puppies insist that their wares are suitable for 'show, work or pet', whether the parents of the litter have any experience in the field or not. Very few individual gundogs, of any breed, have the necessary combination of looks and working ability to succeed in the show ring and the shooting field, though there are exceptions, including some Golden Retrievers.

The first dog I owned was a Golden Retriever. I was too young to have any real involvement with shooting at that time and my first gundog was actually a pet, though he came from working lines. He was, in fact, a gundog reject as, in spite of having an exceptionally gentle nature, he had a mouth like a steel trap where game was concerned. I took him rabbiting as I grew older, but any rabbits that I shot were quickly reduced to pâté as soon as his jaws closed on them. I have no reason to believe that his behaviour was in any way typical of the breed, so do not be put off having a Golden Retriever by my experiences of many years ago. Hard mouth can occur in any gundog of any breed, though some are undeniably more prone to the fault than others. I would not include Golden Retrievers among my list of those which have a strong tendency to hard mouth, since I believe that my old dog was an exception rather than a typical specimen.

The proper, dense coat of the Golden makes them excellent dogs for work in very cold or wet conditions, and affords a measure of protection when they are hunting in thick cover, though there is a natural tendency for a fair amount of the thick cover to attach itself to the coat. Unless you brush all the twigs, burrs, briars and sweethearts out at the end of the day you can soon end up with a badly matted coat that will require major surgery with the scissors in order to tidy it up.

Avoid the temptation to dunk your Golden in the bath at regular intervals. It may be necessary if you want to impress a judge in the show ring, but it is not at all a good thing for a dog which has to swim in freezing water or sit around at a peg on a bitterly cold shoot day. A dog's coat has a naturally oily content which helps to insulate and waterproof the occupant, and regular immersion in detergent-laden water will destroy this protection. Mud will brush out when the coat dries and the dog will groom itself back into respectability given time and a clean, dry kennel.

The Flatcoated Retriever

The origins of the Flatcoat Retriever are not easy to pinpoint, despite a wealth of references to retrievers of various types in nineteenth-century literature. The first Kennel Club register of dogs was published towards the end of the century and listed one 'flatcoated' retriever, forty-seven 'curly-coated' retrievers and one hundred and sixty-two 'wavycoated' retrievers. The register covered the period from 1859 to 1874, and it may be noted that neither Labradors nor Golden Retrievers were listed, though there is no doubt that the foundations of both breeds existed at that time. The wavy-coated soon ceased to be classed as a separate breed and became part of the foundation of today's Flatcoats.

As we saw earlier, there is a great deal of confusion surrounding the retrieving breeds of this period. It is likely that various crosses were tried mixing 'Labrador' blood with setters, collies and hound blood as well as the wavycoated retrievers and that these crosses produced several different types which, by the beginning of the present century, had more or less settled down into the Labrador, the Golden and the Flatcoat Retriever, with the Curlycoat being more directly descended from the old English water dog.

The Flatcoat enjoyed a surge in popularity at the beginning of the century, this commonly being attributed to the work done on the breed by a Mr S. E. Shirley of Ettington Park near Stratford-on-Avon. Mr Shirley, a keen sportsman and gundog breeder, was also a founder of the Kennel Club, a Member of Parliament and a judge of both shows and field trials. With the great driven shoots at their height in the years prior to the First World War, the Flatcoat became the familiar and fashionable companion of the gentleman shot. This popularity survived the war with the Flatcoat becoming the almost automatic choice of the gamekeeper as well as that of his employer. Then, as the first quarter of the century ended, so the numbers of Flatcoats registered with the Kennel Club began to decline until, by the beginning of the Second World War, barely a hundred were registered in the course of one year.

The breed's fortunes began to revive around the start of the fifties, and it is now firmly established as a working breed, though it lags far behind the Labrador and the Golden Retriever in terms of numbers registered annually. Part of this can be attributed to the fact that the Flatcoat does not enjoy the same popularity in the show ring, nor as a house pet, as do the other two breeds, and this should be seen as an asset rather than a liability when looking for a working gundog.

They are typically big, lithe, agile dogs with pace, style and a great affinity with water. Nearly always solid black in colour, with their thick coats and short feathering on the legs, they are exceptionally handsome dogs, stylish in their work and brave when asked to face cover. Their setter ancestors can be seen in several ways: their coats, heads, gait, and quite often in a tendency to point. Quite recently, while out grouse counting with a keeper friend, we saw a trio of black dogs quartering a distant hillside with all the pace and style of a team of pointers or setters. They were getting well out on either flank and working the wind perfectly. Convinced that they must be Gordon Setters, I was astonished when my companion informed me that they were actually Flatcoats. Pace, style and stamina they certainly did not lack.

So why are there not many thousands more Flatcoats in the shooting field? It is always dangerous to speak in general terms, but it is a commonly held view that the Flatcoat is slow to mature, and may well be three years old before it is ready to be introduced to shooting proper. Clearly this does not apply to all Flatcoats, perhaps not even to a majority of Flatcoats, but it is probably true to say that, on average, a Flatcoat is much later to reach maturity than a Labrador.

The Flatcoat is supposed to have a good deal of setter in its make-up, and the essential bouncy good humour of the setter is a characteristic of the Flatcoat's character. As with setters, particularly Irish Setters, this rollicking approach to life can sometimes wear a little thin, particularly where training and early work experience are concerned, and this too may have contributed to the relative lack of popularity of the breed when compared with the Labrador.

Flatcoats are renowned for their courage in water, and in facing thick cover, and make excellent beating and rough shooting dogs once they have matured. As with any gundog it is usually fatal to introduce them to shooting too early, and in the case of the Flatcoat 'too early' could be when the dog is two or even three years old. They have an independence of spirit that is seen less often in the Labrador, and while this will endear them to many owners there are those who will find it trying. That said, a well trained and experienced Flatcoat can be a joy to watch with its elegance and style and the obvious pleasure that it takes in its work.

The Curlycoated Retriever

The fourth of the 'native' retrieving breeds, and by far the least common, is the Curlycoated Retriever. Had I been writing this a hundred and fifty years ago I might well have described the Curlycoat as the most common rather than the least common, but times have changed. Now it is a rare thing to see a Curlycoat in the shooting field, though there are still some working for their living. Their ancestry, according to Stonehenge, is 'always a cross between a St John's Newfoundland and a Water Spaniel, which is generally Irish'. It is well worth quoting a little more of his thoughts on them:

'At present the wavy-coated variety is in fashion, the prevailing opinion being that he is more under control and has a softer mouth. Almost all shooters now depend on a retriever for fetching their game, and as sometimes there are more than half-a-dozen out, their qualities are of considerable importance, especially as time is never allowed for retrievers, and if it is not done at once, the task is given over to the keepers, for otherwise a whole line of shooters would be kept idle, which in the present day would be thought a nuisance. Formerly we used to consider the retrieving of a wounded bird or hare quite as important and interesting as the shooting of others, but all this is changed, and of course we must take the shooting world as we find it. Anyhow, the curly-coated retriever is rare, both on the show bench and in the field, as compared with his numbers fifteen years ago.'

That quote is from an 1879 edition of a book which was originally published in 1859, and the reference to the show bench would suggest that 'fifteen years ago' takes its base from the time of the second edition and means some time around 1865. In the same vein, Mr Teasdale-Buckell wrote, in 1907: 'Forty years ago the curly-coated dogs were the best workers . . .' The decline in popularity was clearly quite rapid, and so complete that by the time the Lonsdale Library published *Hounds and Dogs* in 1943, the Curlycoat no longer rated a mention. And yet a hundred years earlier they had been the most popular of the retrieving breeds.

Perhaps it is significant that they were at their height of popularity at the time when the retriever was first coming into vogue as a result of the growth in driven game shooting following the development of the breech loading shotgun. The early retrievers were bred from water dogs such as the Irish Water Spaniel and the Tweed Spaniel, dogs which were used primarily to retrieve from water, and it was perhaps not surprising that covert shooters soon recognised that ability in water was not a primary requirement of a retrieving dog which was to be used mainly on dry land. The way was open for the Wavycoated Retriever and the various Labrador crosses to grow in popularity at the expense of the Curlycoats.

Writers of the time gave dog shows much of the blame for the decline in the Curlycoat as a working dog, though it is debatable whether the increasing use of Flatcoats and Labradors sprang from a decline in the ability of the Curlies or simply because the developing breeds were better at their work in some way. Certainly the Curlycoat was said to be slower to mature, harder to train and less easy to keep groomed than its rivals. Possibly fashion played a part as well, but whatever the root cause the Curlycoats declined over the latter part of the nineteenth century and have never recovered their status.

They are easily distinguished from the other retrievers by their thick, oily, tightly curled coats which protect them from cold and wet and equip them superbly as wildfowlers' dogs. Like the Flatcoat they are slow to mature and require careful training if they are to show their real ability in the field, but they are highly thought of by those who own and work them. The most difficult thing about working a Curlycoat might well be finding a puppy from working stock, though no doubt this could be done if you were sufficiently determined.

The Chesapeake Bay Retriever

Although the Chesapeake Bay Retriever has been established in America for over one hundred years, the breed has only recently arrived on this side of the Atlantic, the first British Kennel Club registrations being made in 1985.

They are reputed to have originated with a cross between Newfoundlands and Coon Hounds, and are typically big, strong dogs with a dense, almost waterproof, straw-coloured coat. Their forte is water work, and they would appear to be the ideal dog for the wildfowler.

Indeed, it was probably as wildfowlers' dogs that they were originally developed, working with the market gunners of the Chesapeake Bay as well as with those who shot simply for sport. It may seem surprising that they have taken so long to follow the Labrador across the Atlantic, though this may be because wildfowling in Britain was very much a minority sport until quite recently, and never achieved the fashionable status of covert shooting. The Labrador, Flatcoat and Golden Retrievers are all as much at home on land as in the water, perhaps more so, whereas the Chessie is primarily a water dog.

Whatever the reason, they are here now, and the future growth of the breed as working dogs will obviously depend on a sufficient number of enthusiasts breeding, owning and working them.

The Nova Scotia Duck Tolling Retriever

Another retriever that is very much at home in the water is the Nova Scotia Duck Tolling Retriever, of which a few have been brought into the country. They are a medium-sized, reddish-brown dog with a happy, foxy face and a very lively disposition, and I suspect that they may well become very popular, though perhaps more as pets than as gundogs.

They are used in Canada both to decoy and to retrieve wildfowl. The hunter stays hidden from view in a duck blind while the dog cavorts on the bank. Curiosity brings the duck down to investigate, and in this case, curiosity can affect ducks in much the same way as it is supposed to affect cats. I cannot claim to have seen one of these attractive looking little retrievers actually at work, but I will admit to being very taken by the look of the few that I have seen. Hopefully I may get the chance to see one in action some day.

Retriever Work

At first sight retriever work might seem to need little elaboration. You shoot something, the dog goes and retrieves it. What could be simpler? At its most basic retriever work can indeed be as simple as that, though even a 'simple' retrieve can get quite complicated at times. The something that you shoot may not be dead when it hits the ground; it may elect, quite reasonably, to run away, and then the simple retrieve is a simple retrieve no longer.

If your shooting takes place primarily at formal, driven shoots then you will almost certainly be using your dog as a non-slip retriever – that is to say you will expect the dog to sit beside you at your peg or in your butt until the end of each drive, and then to collect any game that you have shot. The best trained and disciplined dogs will indeed sit patiently until the drive is over and only start collecting shot game when ordered to do so; less reliable dogs may be – should be – secured by a lead and some form of ground tackle until the end of the drive. Less reliable dogs which are not secured can be a considerable nuisance, stealing game from the other guns, tempting the steady retrievers to abandon their posts and join in the free for all, and generally confusing the pick-up by lifting birds which other guns have marked down. In general, this is probably the simplest of retriever work since, as Stonehenge observed long ago, if the shooting day is to run according plan there is limited time between drives for the guns' dogs to pick-up. The easy birds – those that are lying close to the pegs – will be collected, but the runners and the lightly pricked birds will probably be left for the pickers-up.

Picking-up is the professional side of the retrieving work done at a driven shoot. The shoot organisers will have planned a certain number of drives to take place within a limited timespan, and there will only be so long between each drive for the guns' retrievers to do their work. You may be willing to spend an hour while your dog hunts out a wounded bird but the other guns and the beaters may get a little fractious after a while, especially if it means losing a couple of drives at the end of the afternoon. The picking-up team will carry on hunting for the difficult birds while the guns and beaters get on with the main business of the day. During the drive they will probably have been watching proceedings from well behind the guns, marking those birds which fly on, although wounded, and drop, or land, back out of sight of the guns themselves.

An experienced retriever can develop what seems like a psychic ability to tell when a bird has been hit. Every regular picker-up will have a story about a dog that was watched a seemingly missed bird land three or four fields away, taken out after it, and returned half an hour later with a wounded pheasant. The chances are that the story will be true. Whether they hear the shot striking the bird, or can tell by some slight difference in the flight, or simply 'know' instinctively when a bird is wounded, there is no doubt that many retrievers can tell that a bird has been hit even when, to our eyes, it is in rude health and totally unmarked by shot or shell. This level of skill is not taught by the trainer, but is developed by the dog through lots of practical experience. Some dogs never develop it; others seem to pick it up in no time.

Picking-up on a big shoot is one of the pinnacles of retrieving work. Pheasants can only be driven in the direction in which they want to fly. In practice, they are often herded, or fed, into a particular spot, then flushed in the expectation that they will head back to the pen in which they were originally released. At the end of the drive it is quite possible that there will be one or two wounded birds running about in the area of the pen with several, or several hundred, birds which are unharmed but tired, and reluctant to fly again unless they are absolutely forced to do so. The picking-up dog will be expected to get into the pen, among those several hundred pheasants, and collected the one, or two, or three which have actually been shot and wounded. The dog will have to distinguish blood scent on the wounded birds and separate them out from among all the others. It may sound impossibly hard, but in fact any good retriever can do it, with experience, and hundreds of them do. We will not say too much at this stage about those that will happily pick-up wounded and unwounded alike, beyond observing that, on some shoots, the guns may be credited with marksmanship above and beyond their actual success rate.

But of course, not all shoots are formal, driven shoots. There are plenty of retrievers employed at rough shoots, by pigeon decoyers, wildfowlers, and beaters, and as flushing dogs while walking-up. Some of those functions, particularly beating, are not strictly retriever work, though since they are all tasks performed regularly by retrieving breeds we should still include them in this section.

The picking-up dog is asked to hunt for dead or wounded game and collect it, while ignoring game that has not been wounded. In case that isn't difficult enough, a beater's dog may be required to take things a step further and hunt out and flush unwounded birds at one moment, then pick-up wounded birds at the next. The dog has to make a value judgement on the basis of scent alone, then decide if the bird, scented but probably unseen, is to be flushed untouched or grabbed before it can run off. Again, this may sound extremely difficult, but in practice there are thousands of good, reliable beating dogs that do this, week in and week out, at shoots all over the country. Sensing when a bird has been pricked by shot and discriminating between wounded and unwounded game are skills that a retriever will learn with experience. The actual action of retrieving is something that the dog will do instinctively. Carrying food back to the den is natural to wolves in the wild, and that instinctive behaviour has been refined and reinforced through generations of breeding to manifest itself particularly strongly in the retrieving breeds. Other behaviour patterns, though, have to be taught to the dog as opposed to being learned through experience or inherited.

Any retriever from working stock will probably retrieve, given that there is something for it to retrieve. If you have spent some time applying basic training principles so that the dog will sit, stay and come to you on command, then you will have a dog that you can use in the field. There are plenty of working retrievers that perform entirely to their owners' satisfaction with no more training than that, and quite a few that satisfy their owners (though perhaps not their owners' companions) without even the basic disciplines being acquired.

There is, though, a lot more that a dog can be taught, and a lot more that you may well insist on your dog learning before you would consider it a finished shooting dog. Any retriever will go and collect a bird that it has seen drop, but what if you have dropped half a dozen birds in half a dozen different places? Do you want your retriever to mark, and remember, where each of those birds fell, and then go out and retrieve them systematically? Or perhaps you have two birds down, a dead bird lying in plain view twenty yards from the peg, and one which you suspect is a runner that fell in the edge of the wood a couple of hundred yards away to your right. You would like the dog to go and hunt for the runner while you stroll across and pick the dead bird. Unless you have trained the dog to collect the bird that you send it for the chances are that it will go and fetch the easy one first, which will give the runner that much more time to get away.

Another scenario. Your neighbour, who doesn't have a dog, shot a grouse which towered and fell 'stone dead' (he says) about half a mile away across the moor, just by one of those peat hags which you can see on the horizon. You could walk across there with your dog and look for it. Better still, with the right training you should be able to send your dog after that bird and guide it with whistle and hand signals right to the spot where the bird should be. If you are going to compete in field trials you will probably consider the foregoing as minimum requirements for your dog. Conversely, if you spend all your shooting days decoying pigeons you may be quite happy if your retriever will simply go and collect any dead birds when you untie him from the spike to which his lead is lashed. Perhaps your shooting days are spent in the beating line rather than at the blunt end of a gun. You want your dog to hunt and flush live game, and perhaps not retrieve at all. An easier task for the dog perhaps? It may be, but then again, consider this. There are driven shoots which release birds by the thousand into their coverts. As the drive develops there might be several hundred pheasants milling about in the last acre or two of cover, nervous, agitated and nearly ready to fly. What the keeper will require here is a steady, controlled flush, putting the birds over the guns a few at a time. What he most definitely will not want is your dog charging in among the pheasants like a thing possessed and sending the whole lot up in one big cloud. A steady, disciplined approach with the minimum of excitement is needed, and woe betide you if your dog doesn't have it. So a beater's dog needs to be cool, calm and very, very steady.

Except sometimes, when it doesn't. Suppose you are at a different shoot, where you and half a dozen others take it in turn to beat or shoot at each drive. You release a hundred birds each year and they spread out over the thousand acres of commercial forestry that comprise your shoot. Now you want the dog to get out and work like a fool to find the two or three pheasants that might, just might, be in this particular block of trees, and harry them hard enough to make them get up and fly instead of exercising their preferred option of running. This isn't the place for dignity and restraint and close control; you won't be able to see the dog through the tightly packed trees anyway. Turn it loose and let it get on with it may be your best bet here, but it is still beating, albeit a different type of beating to the previous shoot, and it requires a good dog to do the job properly. If it is a really good dog then it will be able to do both jobs, depending on which shoot you are working on that day.

There is plenty of variety for the working retriever, and only you can know just what work you are going to ask your dog to undertake. Of the five retrieving breeds you should find it very easy to find a working-bred Labrador, not at all difficult to locate a working Golden or Flatcoat Retriever, and possible, with difficulty, to find a breeder who can sell you a working Curlycoat or Chesapeake Bay Retriever. Logic says that you would be best advised to buy one of the first three, and that for most purposes a Labrador would be the best bet from among them, but you may have a particular whim for one of the others. If so, then do indulge your fancy, but do ensure that whatever your choice of retriever, common old Labrador or rarely seen Curlycoat, it comes from working stock.

And have fun.

Pointers and Setters

The pointers and setters – the bird-dogs, as they are sometimes termed – along with various spaniel breeds have origins which go back much, much further than those of the retrievers. A gentleman called John Harris signed a bond in 1485 in which he undertook to take a spaniel for six months and break it 'to set partridges, pheasants, and other game . . .', for which work he was to receive the sum of 'ten shillings of lawful English money'.

The ability to set or point game – that is, to stop dead at the scent of game and to stay motionless until ordered to move on – is the characteristic that distinguishes the work of the pointing breeds from the other gundogs. It has also been a considerable determinant in the conformation of the breeds, practically all pointing dogs being long-legged when compared to the flushing breeds, and fast moving in comparison with the retrievers. A spaniel, or indeed a retriever, which is used to flush game for the gun must, of necessity, work within gunshot of its handler. In contrast, a dog which will point game, and hold the point without flushing the quarry until the gun has advanced to within shot, can work at a considerable distance from the gun. Clearly, more ground can be covered by such a dog, and clearly, the faster the dog can travel the more ground it can cover and the more game it will find, provided that its nose is equal to the task.

Which leads us to the next requirement of a pointing dog. It has to locate its quarry at a far enough distance so that the quarry will not be panicked into flying or running from the dog. This means that a pointing dog must have a particularly good nose, a nose capable of finding, for example, a single grouse which is fifty yards ahead of it and tucked under a bank of long heather. More than that, it must be capable of finding that grouse while galloping at full speed across the wind, so it must be able to identify it, with certainty, in the fraction of a second that it takes to cross the scent trail carried from that bird by the breeze. Or by a howling gale if it happens to be that sort of day.

So, if we set out to design a bird-dog it would probably be on the lines of a middle distance runner: long on the leg to give it pace, lightly built so that it wasn't lugging any unnecessary poundage around the hill, deep-chested for the stamina that a good set of heart and lungs provides, and possessed of a superbly sensitive nose. And if that all adds up to a pretty fair description of the setters and pointers we have today it is hardly surprising, since they were, in effect, 'designed' for their job by our forebears in the sporting field.

Note that I say 'sporting' rather than shooting, since pointing and setting dogs were used for hunting game long before the introduction of firearms to the sportsman's arsenal. They were used to locate game for the falconer, enabling him to release his falcon into the sky to gain height before the birds were flushed. Pointing dogs are still used by falconers today, the team of birds and dogs operating exactly as they did . . . when? Five hundred years ago certainly; a thousand possibly, and perhaps even before that. Game was also netted in those far-off days before the shotgun took its place in the field, and setters were used to 'sett' game; that is to say, drop down low to the ground when pointing. A net could then be drawn right over both the birds and the dog if the quarry was very close. Pointers, with their more upright stance, are generally supposed to have been less favoured for this kind of work, though I sometimes wonder how accurate this concept is in fact. There are times, certainly, when grouse or partridge will sit so tightly that a net could be dragged over both the birds and the setting dog, but there are other times, too, when the birds are a long way ahead, and a very large net would be required. It would form the basis of a very interesting experiment to try and net some grouse or partridge over a setter as it was supposedly done in days past.

The development of the flintlock first enabled man to use a shotgun for sport in the way that we still use it today. The relatively quick and sure action of the flintlock meant that, for the first time, a man could shoot at a flying bird or a running hare and stand a reasonable chance of killing it. A dog could find the game by its scent, point it to alert the gun to its presence, then rode in and flush it when the gun was in the right position. Once the gun was discharged the dog could be dropped to wait while the gunner went through the slow (by modern standards) process of recharging his gun, then hunt on to find the next covey.

Where game was scarce, or where there was a wide area to hunt, the pointing dogs were the natural choice of the sportsman. Grouse in the heather in August, then partridges among the long stubbles of September and October, followed perhaps by forays after snipe and woodcock on the fens and marshes. There were pointers and setters by the thousand in those days, bred, trained, worked, bought and sold by sportsmen all over the country.

And then the breech loading shotgun was invented. With a breech loading shotgun, or better, with a pair of guns and a loader, the Victorian shot could maintain a rapid firing rate for as long as there were birds to shoot at and cartridges for reloading. Instead of using a dog to hunt for birds which were scarce he could employ keepers to raise pheasants by the thousand and beaters to drive those pheasants over him and his guests. Quite suddenly the retrievers overtook the pointing dogs as the sportsman's indispensable allies, and the art of working bird-dogs was left to that minority of conservative shots who preferred to stick to the old ways. Fortunately there are still some of us around.

The traditional 'British' pointing breeds are the Pointer, the English Setter, the Gordon Setter and the Irish Setter, also known as the Red Setter. There is a fourth category of setter, the Red and White Irish Setter, which you may or may not choose to consider as a breed apart from its Red Setter relations. The setters are all closely related to the spaniels and there are numerous references to 'setting spaniels' in the sporting literature of the Middle Ages. Pointers are a more recent arrival on the scene and are usually said to have developed from imported dogs described as Spanish Pointers, which were heavier and slower than the modern Pointer.

It is difficult to comprehend today just how important the pointing breeds were to the early Victorian sportsman. The first field trials were for pointers and setters. It took another quarter of a century or so for trials for the spaniels and the retrieving breeds to become established. Now, almost a century on, there is something of a revival in the popularity of the bird-dogs both as workers and as competitors in trials. There is no shortage of them in the show ring either, nor as household pets; Irish Setters being the most popular in both roles.

A century and a half ago a pointer or setter was *the* dog for the shooting man. Now they are quite a rare sight in the shooting field, unless you are one of those fortunate individuals who shoot their grouse 'over dogs' each summer. For much of the work required from a shooting man's gundog of today they are, frankly, not suitable, and if you want a non-slip retriever, a wildfowling dog or a hard-hunting flushing dog for rabbiting then I would strongly advise you to put any thought of a pointer or setter out of your mind. On the other hand, if your sporting interests lie in shooting grouse on a sparsely populated Highland hill, hunting woodcock on an extensive chunk of Irish bog or perhaps hunting out a few thousand acres of hill pasture for snipe, then a pointer or setter might be absolutely essential for you. Or, of course, you might just be an enthusiast who loves to see the bird-dogs work, and who will happily travel the length of the country in order to do it. Such enthusiasts do exist – take my word for it.

The Pointer

There is a quite well known engraving of a Spanish Pointer by L. Wells, which shows a heavy dog with a broad head and a docked tail, on point in pasture land. The dog, which is very muscular with a thick neck and barrel chest, is unmistakably a Pointer though it is just as unmistakably a different dog to the Pointers of today. Stonehenge describes the Spanish Pointer in some detail, though he begins by saying that it 'is now quite extinct in this country . . .'

It is clear from their size and conformation that the Spanish Pointer would have been a much slower dog than the modern Pointer, and Stonehenge confirms this: '. . . the Spanish Pointer [is] . . . very slow in his gallop, which pace indeed is seldom displayed, a steady trot being the usual one, even when turned off in a large stubble field. Still a brace of these dogs when well broken would quarter a field almost while their master was walking across it, and they would never leave a head of game behind, even on the worst scenting day. I fear this cannot be said of any of our modern breeds, who, it is true, will beat twice as much ground as the Spanish Pointer, in half the time, but in so doing will probably flush a covey or two, or possibly leave a few single birds to get up as soon as the guns are over the gate.' Field trial enthusiasts please note that the passage above was written by Stonehenge in 1859, not by me in 1995.

A great deal of the pleasure to be gained from working pointers and setters comes from watching the dogs. There are few sights in field sports to match that of a brace of Pointers quartering a moor with that pace, style and elegance which should be so characteristic of the breed. The dog which potters about may well find more game than a free running dog – eventually – but the potterer is far less fun to watch at work. Of course, much depends on where you draw the line between 'pottering' and 'free running', and how many missed or flushed birds you are prepared to accept in exchange for the pleasure of watching a fast dog. A good pointer should move with sufficient pace and style to gladden the eye but – and for me this is an important 'but' – it should not run with such abandon that it consistently bumps or misses birds. Pointers and setters must run for the sake of hunting; if they begin to run simply for the sake of running then they cease to be gundogs, and become something which is a cross between a dog show and a greyhound race. If that is your requirement from your bird-dog then fine; you are entitled to enjoy your dog work in whatever form you choose. However, when a demonstration of pace becomes more important than finding game the sport we are considering is no longer primarily concerned with shooting.

The old Spanish Pointer was almost certainly crossed with greyhound and foxhound in order to produce the lighter, faster dog which was required by the shooting men of the day. The resulting dog is commonly referred to as the 'English' Pointer, though this title brings howls of protest from the more formal of Pointer people who insist, quite correctly, that the proper name of the breed is just Pointer. Incidentally, the section on the

Pointer in Stonehenge's book was titled 'The Modern English Pointer', so the fault in nomenclature is not exactly a new one.

The various crosses – bloodhound is sometimes cited as well as foxhound and greyhound – certainly transformed the slow, heavy Spanish dog into something much faster, lighter and more elegant, but certain undesirable traits were introduced along with the good ones. Pointing dogs should hunt with their heads high, seeking always to find their quarry by its body scent, carried to them on the wind. Hounds though are accustomed to use foot scent – the residual scent left after the bird or animal has passed by – and this use of foot scent is anathema to the pointing breeds.

I should perhaps qualify that last statement. My bird-dogs will work foot scent, and there are times when I am more than happy for them to do so. Game birds do not always obligingly sit tight in front of a pointing dog. An old cock grouse running and twisting through a peat hag will probably be lost for ever unless the dog can drop its nose and puzzle out its trail. Pheasants too would often rather run than fly, and a dog which can track them will probably offer the gun his best chance of a shot. There are times when it is acceptable, desirable even, for a pointing dog to track game by foot scent.

But there are also times when it is not acceptable. Pointing dogs should always seek their game initially with their heads held high to catch body scent. The majority do, of course, but there are occasional throwbacks which insist on running with their noses brushing the ground looking for foot scent as their first objective. This was a far more common fault a century ago when the various out-crosses were that much closer in the dogs' ancestry, but it does still occur. A dog which hunts for foot scent is always prone to false pointing – indicating that game is present when there is none – and this can be an infuriating trait, particularly when the 'point' is up a mountain-side, several hundred feet above you and well away from your intended line of march.

When a dog points the gun must go to him. There will not always be birds, since no dog is perfect, but there should be a reasonable expectation that when the dog says 'birds' there will be birds in front of him. Shooting over a dog which persistently points falsely is a very mixed blessing, particularly when you have toiled up the hill for the nth time only to be greeted with a guilty look and a few minutes' non-productive snuffling at the heather.

The Pointer has a short, springy coat which is ideal for working the moors in the heat of an August day but less suitable when days are cold and wet. The colour today is usually a mixture of white and either liver – a rich, dark brown – black, orange or lemon, but whole coloured black Pointers were once fashionable, and some still exist. Early photographs of black Pointers owned by William Arkwright – the author of *The Pointer and His Predecessors*, the standard work on the breed – show their greyhound ancestry very clearly, and this conformation of body and head can still be identified in the whole coloured black Pointers which I have seen. Colour is largely a matter of individual preference, though Stonehenge devoted considerable space to a discussion of which coloured dogs were the best workers. He settled on liver and white, incidentally, though I have personally never felt that colour had any effect whatsoever on working ability.

Pointers tend to take their work seriously, particularly when compared with an Irish Setter, of which more later. It is my own experience that they tend to be ready for work a little sooner than the setters, though having said that I have seen some excellent setters of all breeds, running, and running well, in Puppy Stakes. Where the setters are sometimes a little vague when setting, the sett at times being accompanied by a gently waving tail, there is generally no doubt whatsoever when a Pointer has found birds.

At field trials for pointers and setters the dogs are run as a brace, that is to say two dogs are run at the same time on the same beat. This was the traditional way of running pointing dogs, though it is more common today to run one dog at a time. The old kennels housed dozens, sometimes hundreds, of dogs, and there was no shortage of helpers to lead spare dogs on a shooting day. Two dogs running on the same beat will inevitably cover much of the ground twice and, while this reduces the odds of a bird being missed, it also makes inefficient use of the dogs.

A dog which trots along gently à la Spanish Pointer can, if fit, run all day long. However, when that steady trot is replaced by a racing gallop, the length of time which the dog can reasonably be expected to run will fall accordingly. If you want your pointing dogs to run as pointing dogs should, then you will need more than one dog when you plan a full day in the field. Two is the absolute minimum, working turn and turn about, and if you plan a long day then you will be better served if you have three or four dogs on the team. And if you want to run them as a brace each time you will need twice as many. That said, if there is a better sight in the shooting world than a brace of Pointers, one pointing and the other backing, standing absolutely motionless against a backdrop of hills and heather, then I have yet to see it.

The Irish Setter

The Irish Setter or Red Setter has something of a reputation for wildness – madness some will say – and the admission that we keep Irish Setters is often enough to prompt a horror story of homes and furniture wrecked, marriages broken and owners driven to the verge of suicide. 'But they are beautiful dogs, aren't they?' the story will conclude, and with that at least I can usually concur.

To a large extent it is that beauty – the combination of rich, red coat, graceful, flowing movement and devil-may-care attitude to life – which has contributed to the Irishman's bad reputation. As puppy or adult the Irish Setter is an irresistibly appealing animal, and thousands are bought every year as pets, or show dogs, and then expected to live a lifestyle for which they are far from suited.

The Irish Setter was bred to work: to hunt for grouse, snipe, woodcock and partridge in places were game was scarce; to run effortlessly and endlessly for mile after mile over moor and mountain, eternally optimistic that there would be a bird – or better, a covey – on the very next cast. They were bred to have boundless energy, a love of running and a desire to see what exactly the world is like on the other side of the hill. And we take them, lock them up all day in a flat in Hampstead, then wonder why they become bored, frustrated and sometimes destructive; why they run away and refuse to return after their regular evening turn around the recreation ground. Yes, the Irish Setter has a reputation for wildness, but the fault lies less with the dogs than with those owners who subject them to a lifestyle better suited to a Pug or a Peke than to a working gundog.

Even so, the Irish Setter is by far the most common of the pointing breeds, though the vast majority of them are never likely to hear the sound of gunfire. Their popularity as pets and show dogs has seen the breed split into two types: the workers and the rest, of which the rest are in the majority.

It was perhaps natural that non-working breeders would select the more manageable of their stock to produce future generations, just as the show fraternity breed for looks rather than working ability. As a result there are lots of beautiful and relatively placid Irish Setters about which do indeed make reasonable pets, but which lack the fire and the drive needed if they are to be reasonable workers. I should add that this situation is by no means limited to Irish Setters, but the popularity enjoyed by the breed in the early 1970s has meant that there are an awful lot of non-working Irish Setters about – which is fine, unless you are looking for one to work, in which case you must take care to get one from working lines.

The normal colour of the Irish Setter is a rich, chestnut red, sometimes with a white spot on the chest, head or toes. In the last twenty years or so there has been a revival of red and white coloured Irish Setters, and they are now recognised as a separate breed by the Kennel Club, though I would personally be more inclined to consider the Red and White Setter as simply a colour variation of the Red Setter, just as the Pointers, English and Gordon Setters are accepted in different colour combinations. In fact, Red and White Setters are probably closer to the original Irish Setter than the whole coloured dogs which are so familiar today.

The setters were commonly referred to in the past as 'setting spaniels' and it is to the spaniels that we must look in order to trace the origins of the Irish Setter and his cousins. Stonehenge is at pains to point out that the setters were trained to sett, whereas the pointing instinct was more deeply ingrained in the Spanish Pointer which preceded the Pointer. This may or may not be the reason why some setters are less steady than pointers; certainly Stonehenge thought it was so. 'As a rule the setter is faster than the pointer, but not so steady, frequently requiring a day or two's work before he can be relied upon.' There is not very much that I would want to add to that statement.

My own experience with Irish Setters is that they tend to take longer than a Pointer to mature and to train. Where the Pointer tends to take his work seriously the Irish Setter takes a much more light-hearted view of things. When one of our Pointers flushes a bird by accident it will usually look shame-faced and apologetic. In contrast I have seen more than one Irish Setter which will occasionally flush a covey just for the hell of it, then come back grinning from ear to ear to accept whatever is handed out in the way of retribution. 'I know I shouldn't have done it, but it was fun.'

In the same way a Pointer, once trained, is normally trained for life. True, at the start of the season he will need to be got fit, and to be reminded of his manners before starting work in earnest, but what gundog does not? Irish Setters though, or certainly the majority of the Irish Setters I have worked with and shot over, have a tendency to need retraining at the start of each new season. Not the full works from the beginning of course, but they certainly need more time spent on them than do the Pointers.

The Irish Setter, like the English and the Gordon Setters, has a longer coat than the Pointer, with feathering on legs, chest and tail. This longer coat is often said to make them less suitable than the Pointer for work on hot days, though I have never found any of our Irish Setters to be adversely affected by the heat to a greater extent than the Pointers. Certainly they love water, and will wallow in any wet pool given the chance, but so will the Pointers if the day is warm. At the other extreme, the Irish Setter is certainly far happier than the Pointer when the weather is wet or cold. I remember a field trial at Snake Pass on the Pennines when the rain was driving across the moor in horizontal sheets. Most of the dogs and handlers had taken to what shelter could be found in the lee of a peat hag, but our young Irish Setter bitch was standing quite happily facing into the teeth of the gale, seemingly quite impervious to the cold and the wet. She was not the most intelligent of dogs, so it is possible that she hadn't noticed the weather, but I think the truth is that she simply didn't care.

The English Setter

Like their Irish cousins the English Setters are generally accepted to have descended from spaniel stock, their setting instincts being developed by selective breeding over many generations. In fact, to say that they are descended from spaniels is a little misleading, since the spaniels themselves were being refined and developed at the same time as the setters, so a more accurate assessment might be that the spaniels and setters have been selectively bred from common ancestors.

While the Irish were breeding their red, or red and white coloured setters, breeders in England, Scotland and Wales were developing a number of different strains of setting dog. One of the most influential of the breeders, Edward Laverack, wrote a book entitled *The Setter* in 1872 in which he listed eleven different types of setter. Of these the Gordon Setter and the Irish Setter still remain as separate breeds, the Russian Setter and the Welsh Setter are no longer recognised in Britain, and the remaining seven are amalgamated into the modern English Setter. Some authorities still sub-divide the English Setter into two types – the Laverack, named after Edward Laverack, and the Llewellin, named after a Mr Purcell Llewellin who, with Laverack, was instrumental in developing the breed. At least, this is the generally accepted view, though writers of the latter part of the nineteenth century do not give the same weight to the work of these two breeders as is the current vogue. In America the Llewellin is recognised as a separate type, though this is not the case in Britain. We do though have two types of English Setter – the show type and the working type – and the difference between them is more pronounced in English Setters than in any of the other pointing breeds.

Show type English Setters are beautiful, elegant animals, but they are completely different in their appearance from the working strains which are smaller and less well feathered with an entirely different head, and an entirely different attitude to life. Show-bred English Setters may make excellent companions and house pets but they are simply not equipped for the shooting field, lacking the drive which is essential if they are to find birds, and reputedly lacking the ability to handle them if by some chance they do make contact with a covey. It is not the case that the show dogs conform to the breed standard while the working strains have been allowed to degenerate through selection for working ability alone. Photographs of English Setters taken around the turn of the century show dogs which closely resemble the working dogs of today, and it is the show breeders who have strayed away from the proper conformation, coat and character of the breed. After which I need hardly add the usual rider that you should only buy your English Setter puppy from true working lines, unless you want to show the dog, in which case you must buy from show stock and abandon any thoughts of shooting over it.

At work the English Setter has much in common with its Irish cousins, and is similarly said to be better under wet conditions than it is when the weather is hot and dry. When setting they commonly stand with their head and tail both held high, making a characteristically elegant curve along their top line. The breed is prone to stickiness – showing a reluctance to rode forward when required. This fault can occur with any pointing dog, though the English Setter does have a particularly bad reputation for it. At its simplest it may just mean that the dog will occasionally be reluctant to move in to birds once it has pointed, but can be persuaded by a nudge from the handler, or perhaps by the handler crossing in front of the dog and causing a momentary break in the scent. At its worst the dog will be physically incapable of movement and the only option is for the handler to go forward and flush the birds himself.

A mildly sticky dog is little more than a nuisance, unless you are a field trial competitor, and may make a perfectly satisfactory shooting dog. A dog with a really bad case of stickiness can be almost useless. There will be times when it won't matter, days when the birds are jumpy and get up without the dog having to rode in; but there will also be times when it is a real headache. Perhaps the worst thing about a sticky dog is that you can't tell if it is going to be sticky until it is pretty well advanced in its training. Indeed, stickiness may well develop in a dog, and a formerly free-moving dog may become sticky, possibly because the fault was there waiting to surface, though it is also possible to induce stickiness through bad training. If a dog is treated harshly in order to make it drop to flush it is possible that it will associate punishment with the act of lifting its birds. The result? The dog refuses to move in. Logically, if you can induce stickiness you should also be able to cure it, provided that the fault was the result of poor training and not an inbred trait.

The working English Setter has seemed to enjoy something of a revival in the last few years. On the field trial circuit there are not only more English Setters running but there are some very good ones among them. This is not simply fortuitous, but the result of a lot of hard and dedicated work by several real enthusiasts of the breed. Fortunes and fashion do at times appear to follow a cycle among the pointer and setter field trialling breeds, and it is good to see the fortunes of the English Setter rising again.

The Gordon Setter

There is a story, almost certainly apocryphal, that the Gordon Setter has its origins in a shepherd's collie dog that was used as a pointing dog by the Duke of Gordon. Slightly more credible, but still unlikely, is the idea that the Gordon developed as the result of a collie cross being introduced into the Duke's kennel. In fact, it seems more likely that Alexander, 4th Duke of Gordon, simply had a preference for the black and tan dogs and implemented his breeding policy accordingly.

The Duke was certainly not the only breeder of black and tan setters, and during the latter part of the last century classes at dog shows were for 'Black and Tan Setters' rather than for Gordon Setters. Stonehenge says: 'After a lengthened controversy, it is now generally admitted that the Gordon Setter was originally white, black and tan, and that many black and tan setters are not descended from the Gordon Castle kennels.' However, the breed is now known as the Gordon Setter, and the dogs are coloured predominantly a deep, rich black with tan markings on their faces, chests and legs. The show standard allows only a small white spot on the chest, which seems a strange anomaly in view of the fact that the dogs may well have originally been tricoloured. It is fortunate that this colour blindness does not extend to the working dog or field trial enthusiasts would have been denied the pleasure of seeing Mr Bob Truman's first-class tricoloured dog which won the Champion Stake in 1980.

The Gordon is bigger and heavier than the other setters, and in the past was always rated as a slower dog in its work. Their size, weight and colouring is sometimes attributed to bloodhound ancestry, though this is as firmly denied by some experts as it is propounded by others. Captain L. C. R. Cameron, writing in the Lonsdale Library's 1943 edition of *Hounds and Dogs*, described the Gordon at work as 'plodding' and 'painstaking', though he did not intend the terms as a slight. Let me quote the Captain in a little more detail:

'The Gordon Setter is the most handsome and most workmanlike of all British gundogs; and for its especial work on "dogging moors" among grouse, blackgame and ptarmigan there is no setter or pointer to equal it. Not only does it withstand the extreme heat of August better than any light-coloured dog, but it will work longer and more perseveringly without water than other setters. These undeniably good qualities are due to its stamina, staunchness and nose, which result in that plodding, painstaking work for the love of work, eliminating every possible chance of error, that characterises not only this typically Scottish dog, but also its human countryfellows as a race. For this reason the shooting-man obsessed by a false idea of economising time – the chief blot on the modern system of judging pointer and setter field trials – has dubbed the Gordon Setter an "old man's dog"; an intended term of reproach that might be altered to "the sensible sportsman's dog", when it is employed in its proper work on a "dogging moor".'

The modern Gordon Setter, and certainly those that are running in field trials at this time, could never be described as slow or plodding, and will match the pointers and the other breeds of setter for pace. This is no doubt due to a speeding up on behalf of the Gordons rather than any slowing down on the part of the other breeds. That it is a good thing as far as field trial results go is undeniable, since some trial judges place such an emphasis on pace alone that they will eliminate 'slow' dogs which find birds while lamenting that 'all the good dogs' – i.e. the faster dogs – 'were unlucky and either flushed or missed birds'. Whether it is as good for the Gordons as a breed is open to question, since there is undoubtedly a place for a dog which can run all day, albeit at a slower pace.

Pointer and Setter Work

It is not for nothing that the pointers and setters are often referred to as 'bird-dogs', for it is the finding of game birds that is the whole reason for their existence. Dogs that pointed or sett their quarry were used by sportsmen long before the invention of the gun, the game that they found being netted, flushed for a falcon to fly down or, in the case of hares, to be coursed by greyhounds. As developments in the making of firearms made shooting birds on the wing a viable proposition, so the setters and pointers were adapted to hunt game for the shotgunner.

Grouse and partridge were the main quarry in those days, followed by snipe and woodcock and, of course, the pheasant, though pheasants, with their propensity to run rather than hide, were not, and are not, the ideal quarry for bird-dogs. Grouse and partridge, snipe and woodcock all rely for their protection on not being seen by their predators. To this end they have developed superbly camouflaged plumage and the ability to crouch motionless in the lowest of cover and still be virtually invisible to the eye of hawk or human.

Invisible they may be, but they cannot disguise their scent, and it is the scent of the game that all gundogs work on, retrievers and spaniels as well as the pointing breeds. A dog will locate its quarry by the scent of the quarry alone; a good pointing dog will do so from such a distance that the quarry will remain in its hiding place in the belief that the dog is not yet close enough to present any immediate danger. Let the dog move in closer though and the bird will fly, or the hare will run, trusting that a sudden, explosive appearance will disconcert the dog long enough to give it the head start which it needs to allow it to escape.

The art of pointer work is for the dog to find birds that are widely scattered – so widely scattered that it would be futile for a gun to try and walk them up alone, or with a dog working within gunshot as a flushing dog must – to point them when it finds them, and to hold that point without flushing them until the gun has got into position to shoot, and only then to flush the game. Bird-dog work in a nutshell, and at times it really is as simple as that. Such a simple description though can hardly do justice to the

Top: Worried look from this Gordon Setter puppy.

Above left: The Curlycoated Retriever was one of the most popular retrieving dogs at the end of the last century, but few are seen working these days.

Above right: Clumber Spaniel; the biggest of the spaniel breeds and a thorough, if somewhat steady, worker.

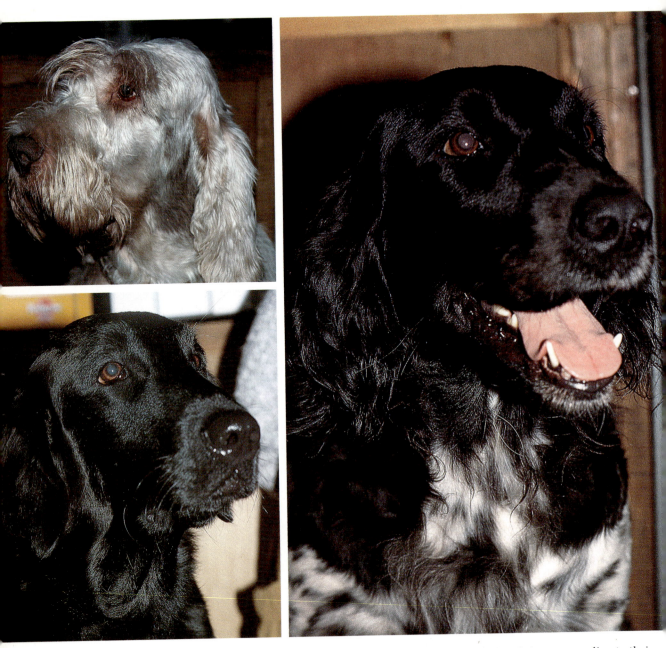

Top left: Hunt, Point and Retrieve Field Trial judges are required to assess dogs like this Italian Spinone according to their particular style of work rather than comparing them directly with the faster, wider ranging dogs.

Above left: Flatcoated Retriever. Being slower to mature than the Labrador may account for the Flatcoat's relatively low numbers in the shooting field.

Above right: The Large Munsterlander is closely related to the German Longhaired Pointer, a breed which has not yet found a niche in Britain.

Below left: This Irish Setter puppy may look soft and cuddly, but it will grow up into a fast-running, hard-working hunting dog.

Below right: The Nova Scotia Duck Tolling Retriever – a lively and appealing little dog that will surely increase in popularity among wildfowlers.

Bottom: The English Springer, like the Labrador, can be found wherever there is shooting sport to be enjoyed.

Top left: Field Spaniels were once common, though the name was also used as a general term for 'land' spaniels, but are rarely seen working now.

Top right: Typical working Cocker Spaniel head, which is quite distinct from the appearance of the show-bred Cockers.

Above: Cocker Spaniel pausing briefly in the course of a day spent in the beating line.

Opposite: Relaxing for a moment on a sunny autumn day on the moors.

Above left: Hungarian Vizslas. Lively and athletic, but generally a much 'softer' dog than the other Hunt, Point and Retrieve breeds.

Top right: The Kooikerhondje is a lively and intelligent little dog, used in its native Holland as a 'piper' in duck decoys.

Bottom right: Goshawk on the fist. Long before the development of the shotgun the ancestors of the modern gundogs were employed to flush game for falconers.

Top left: This Irish Water Spaniel is not only a very handsome dog but it is regularly worked both as a picking-up and a beating dog.

Top right: German Shorthaired Pointer. The most popular working dog among the Hunt, Point and Retrieve breeds.

Above: The danger of a dog that runs in. The gun has killed the grouse, but only good fortune has prevented the dog from being peppered as well.

Opposite: Cocker Spaniel puppy.

pleasure of a day in the field, shooting 'over dogs'.

In no other form of shooting is the work of the dog so important. On a grouse moor in August, particularly the type of ground that is generally described as a 'dogging moor', which means one with a low density of grouse, you might walk all day without a dog and never see a grouse. The young grouse are not yet strong enough on the wing to stand a chance of eluding a peregrine or harrier, so they sit tightly; so tightly that it is often possible to pick them up if you can spot them among the heather. It is certainly possible to walk right through the middle of a covey and never suspect that they are there. Take a good bird-dog, though, and you will know where the grouse are hiding, because the dog will point them for you. And because the dog should hold that point until you tell him to get on, he can point birds which are far out of range of your gun. All you have to do is to walk over to the dog, in you own time, and then tell him to get on and flush the birds once you are in position. Oh yes, and then you have to shoot straight, but that is your problem, not the dog's.

In between points you get to watch the dogs at work. Now, there are some people who take little pleasure in watching a pointer or a setter quartering a moor or a stubble field. If all you see is a dog running about then shooting over dogs is probably not the sport for you. On the other hand, if you can take pleasure in the very action of the dog running – watch and try to interpret each little nuance of the dog's attitude; see how his gait changes as he draws in to the scent of game; try and anticipate what the dog is telling you when he points – then you will almost certainly enjoy the experience, even if you don't shoot a lot of grouse or partridge in the course of the day. Shooting over dogs is all about dog work, just as hunting, for many a hunt follower, is all about watching the hounds at their job. There is a great deal to admire in the way a pointer or setter flows across the ground with a seemingly effortless pace that makes light of hills and hags. There is a fascination in seeing the way that the dog adapts its pattern to every little change in the wind. If you happen to be running a brace of dogs then there is no better sight than one dog pointing and another backing while the guns and the handler stride quietly across the stubble or the heather towards them.

Backing – where one dog comes on to point and its brace-mate then points at the pointing dog – is a necessary trait if more than one dog is to run at one time. If one dog points and another tries to steal the point – come up alongside, or past the pointing dog – then jealously may cause one or both dogs to go in and flush the quarry prematurely. Backing means that the non-finding dog stays behind, or to one side of, the pointing dog, and does not interfere with the working out of the point. It does not, as is so often stated in gundog books, give the guns a cross-reference on the position of the quarry. Only one dog, the pointing dog, will normally have the scent of the birds, unless the backing dog is directly downwind from it. The back is induced by the dog seeing the stationary form of its running mate. Sometimes a back may be induced by a stationary sheep, a tree stump or a white stone, and can cause a little false excitement, since although the dog thinks it is backing another dog you, knowing that the other dog is not in front on point, are liable to assume that the back is in fact a point. You will usually realise the error when you arrive at the white stone, the sheep or the tree trunk, or when the dog realises its mistake and breaks off its 'point'.

The work of the pointing dog is often said to end at the moment when the quarry is flushed. Many handlers do not allow their bird-dogs to retrieve, and there are sound arguments in favour of this. It is said that anticipation of the retrieve can make the dogs unsteady and liable to run in, that having found the birds the pointing dog deserves a rest while the retriever does its work, and that pointers and setters are unsuitable to work as retrievers. With the first two points I have some sympathy; the third is nonsense and can be dismissed as such immediately.

In Britain it has become accepted among many gundog enthusiasts that pointers and setters do not retrieve, and in many cases this is correct, because their handlers do not require or allow them to do so. At field trials, which are normally run during the close season, there is no requirement for retrieving, since no game will be shot. When the guns have their own specialist retrievers as well as bird-dogs they may prefer that the retrievers do the retrieving. Their bird-dogs will therefore not retrieve, but they will not retrieve because they are not required to, not because they cannot, or will not. The setters are, after all, descended from the same, basic stock as the spaniels, and there is setter blood in at least one retrieving breed, the Flatcoat. In the days before the retrieving breeds had attained their popularity there were no specialist retrievers, and which dogs should we assume did the retrieving then? Obviously, the pointers and setters, as they still do on the Continent and in America, and as they will here if you require it of your bird-dogs.

Anticipating the command to retrieve can certainly make a dog unsteady, but it can do the same for a spaniel or a retriever. There is some credence in the 'give the dog a break' argument, and there may be a case for resting the pointing dog while the specialist does the picking up. However, having seen just how keen many pointers and setters are to retrieve, I would doubt if the dogs themselves would prefer the break to the chance of finishing off the job properly. And finally, if it is such a problem to allow a pointing dog to retrieve, why are the Hunt, Point and Retrieve breeds becoming so popular? Let me emphasise that I am not suggesting that a bird-dog is a suitable substitute for a retriever to sit at a peg on a driven shoot or to crouch in a muddy gutter on the foreshore waiting for a goose to drop into the tide. Bird-dogs are not retriever substitutes. However, there is no reason why they should not be used to retrieve as part of their normal work, provided that you want them to do it.

Neither are they suited for spaniel work, close hunting in thick cover or working in the beating line where pheasants by the hundred are milling about in a wood. Their place is out running on the moor, the snipe bog or the autumn stubbles, hunting for game that is scarce and elusive. Beware though of trying to work a pointing dog in front of a line of guns. It is a common misconception that the guns should walk in line when using a bird-dog, just as if they were walking up grouse or partridge. This is not only wrong, it is sometimes dangerous and invariably confusing for the dog, which is used to working a beat to either side of its handler. If the guns walk along spread out across a couple of hundred yards of moor, the dog may well try to quarter a beat on either side of the line, i.e. take in more and more ground as the line widens, unless the handler walks in clear sight, well ahead of the line of guns. You may agree to walk across rough ground with a line of loaded guns at your back; I prefer not to do so.

The proper way to shoot over dogs is much simpler, much safer, and much more fun than trying to maintain a disciplined line across country while carrying a loaded gun and anticipating a shot at any moment. First and foremost, you accept that it is the dog's job to find birds, and the dog's job to stop and point when he finds them. If the birds sit and the dog stays then you will have plenty of time to walk across to the point and load your gun when you get there, so you can carry it open and empty until there is a point. You can chat to your fellow gun as you walk, but please do so quietly – birds have ears, and at times they are easily frightened.

Two is the ideal number of guns for shooting over dogs. When the dog points you advance one on either side of the dog, and a few yards ahead. The attitude of the dog on point – the angle of his head, the eagerness with which he moves forward – can give you a good idea of where the birds are; how far in front, running or sitting tightly. Get into the right position, and try to stay in position as the dog rodes forward. An old cock grouse running through the heather can twist and turn like a snake, and you must try and anticipate where it is going to rise from then move accordingly. The birds may jump from right under your feet and need to be allowed a little law before you mount the gun, or they may flush forty or fifty yards ahead of the dog and offer only the most fleeting of chances before they are out of range. But it wouldn't be any fun if it was too easy.

Pointers and setters are not for everyone. There is little point in getting a bird-dog if what you really need is a spaniel, or a specialist retriever. You can work a pointer or setter in the beating line, but the other dogs will quickly learn to spot when the dog is pointing and to nip in and flush the quarry, which is a sure way to make a dog unsteady. But if you do have access to a grouse moor, or to open fields with partridges or snipe, or if you want to have a crack at the pointer and setter trial circuit, then one of the bird-dogs might be just the thing for you. Though of course, if you are thinking about doing the job as it should be done you will want two, or three or four of them to make up a team and do the job properly.

Spaniels

The spaniels are among the oldest of the gundog breeds. There are numerous references to them in medieval records, and dogs which are recognisably spaniels are often shown in paintings from the past. Their influence can be seen in many of today's gundogs, including setters and retrievers, as well as in the modern spaniel breeds.

Although there are plenty of references in ancient literature to spaniels in general, it is not a simple task to unravel the background of the various breeds that are recognised today. Several writers have tried, and there are a number of different authorities which claim that this breed or that breed is the original spaniel, or that the lines of another breed have been kept pure for the last several hundred years, and it is entirely possible that one or more of those writers may be correct. At the same time it is quite certain that they cannot all be correct, and I have no way of knowing for certain which, if any, of the 'authorities' is the real authority.

Today there are seven recognised breeds of working spaniel: the English Springer, Welsh Springer, Cocker, Clumber, Sussex, Field and Irish Water Spaniels, plus the American Cocker which is primarily a show or pet dog, and therefore outside my remit. Those seven breeds have been established and accepted for most of the current century, and their ancestry can be traced back to the beginning of the century through pedigree records for those of you who might wish to occupy themselves in this way. Prior to that, though, the classification of the various spaniel types becomes a little clouded.

Stonehenge divided the breeds initially into Field Spaniels and Water Spaniels, then sub-divided them further. Note particularly that 'Field Spaniel' as used by Stonehenge refers to a group of gundogs and not to a particular breed, as it does today. He says: 'A great variety of these dogs [Field Spaniels] exists throughout Great Britain, and, until lately, they were divided into large spaniels (springers) and small (cockers). Nowadays, however, only four distinct varieties are acknowledged, viz – (a) the Clumber; (b) the Sussex; (c) the Norfolk; and (d) the modern cocker.' According to Stonehenge, then, the designation Springer Spaniel had fallen into disuse by 1879 when he revised the earlier (1859) edition of his work. In direct contrast, a later writer, Dorothy Morland-Hooper, cites the records kept by a Shropshire family called Boughey who have a stud book of Springer Spaniels which runs unbroken from 1813 to the 1930s.

The Norfolk Spaniel has since disappeared as a separate breed, and in effect been absorbed into the ranks of the Springers. The Field Spaniel is now accepted as a breed in its own right rather than a general classification for 'land spaniels', and the Welsh Springer, which Stonehenge referred to in passing as the 'Welsh Cocker', is one of those breeds whose proponents claim ancient and unbroken lineage back to the year dot.

Until the early years of this century the dividing line between Springers and Cockers was one of weight. Spaniels weighing less than twenty-eight pounds were Cockers, heavier ones were Springers. It was quite possible therefore for a single litter to produce both Springer and Cocker progeny, for two Springers to be mated and produce Cocker pups, and vice versa. Indeed, the first English Springer Field Trial Champion was Rivington Sam, a dog whose parents were a Springer dog, Spot of Hagley, and a Cocker bitch, Rivington Riban. This mating was quite acceptable to the Kennel Club at that time, though you might find it a little difficult to get a registration for a similar combination today.

The situation with regard to what Stonehenge called Water Spaniels was not quite so confused, though he did divide the Irish Water Spaniel into two classifications – the Irish Water Spaniel (as used in the south) and the Northern Irish Water Spaniel. The English Water Spaniel was dismissed in relatively few words as 'a very indefinite character; nearly all that can be said of him being that he is a large, curly, liver-and-white spaniel, used for wildfowl shooting'.

There was clearly a lot of mixing and matching among the various types of spaniel during the nineteenth and early twentieth centuries, and it is difficult to form a clear picture of how the various breeds, as we now recognised them, were developed. It is generally accepted though that the name 'spaniel' was originally bestowed because the dogs originated in Spain. Whatever their origins, the spaniels were used, as they are still used, to hunt for game and flush it for the sportsman; sportsmen in those days being falconers, owners of coursing dogs or hunters netting game for the table. With the development of the sporting shotgun the spaniels began to be used to hunt and flush game for the shooting man, and that has remained their role to the present day.

In the early days of shooting for sport the spaniels would have been used both as hunters of live game, which they would flush for their handlers to shoot, and as retrievers when the shot was successful, sport which would be close to the rough shooting at which they excel today. When driving game became the fashion some spaniels would have been used only for retrieving work, and many a spaniel is still employed primarily as a retriever right to the present day.

There is a huge gulf between working spaniels and those bred for the show bench; indeed that gulf is probably wider in certain of the spaniel breeds than in any other gundogs. This is not by any means a recent development. By 1907 – i.e. only thirty years after Stonehenge's book was published – Teasdale-Buckell was writing of spaniels being 'grotesquely altered by selection for exhibition'. Nothing has happened since to improve the situation, and I have even seen it suggested that the Springers and Cockers should be split into two distinct categories, the working type and the show type. The divergence between working and show dogs is so great that it is quite feasible to categorise dogs as 'workers' or 'show dogs' with no more than a passing glance. Such pigeon-holing sorts them as to their physical appearance, and it is nearly as easy to separate the workers from the show dogs by introducing them to a bit of cover and seeing how they would hunt it through. In the spaniel breeds, perhaps more so than with any others, it is absolutely vital that a dog which is wanted for work must come from working lines.

Which brings us round to the question of which breed is the right one for the shooting man. The first thing to say is that, if you are wanting a working spaniel, it is almost certain to be either a Springer or a Cocker. I say 'almost certain' because it is still possible to obtain dogs of working stock from all the other breeds, though their appearance in the shooting field is far from common. If you particularly want a working Clumber, Sussex or Field Spaniel I have no doubt you should be able to locate one, somewhere. If, on the other hand, you simply want a working spaniel, then your choice for all practical purposes is between a Springer and a Cocker.

The English Springer Spaniel

The English Springer – simply referred to as the Springer from here on – is unquestionably the most popular of the working spaniels. There may be a few more Cocker Spaniels registered each year with the Kennel Club, but the proportion of working to non-working dogs is far higher for the Springers than for their smaller cousins. The Labrador is probably the most common of the working dogs, but the Springer will surely run it a close second. Be it a formal driven shoot or a pigeon decoyer's hide, a rough shoot or a grouse moor, a muddy estuary or a sandy rabbit warren, the Springer will be there.

The primary role of the spaniel breeds is to hunt live game and flush it for the guns to shoot. Originally they would have worked in front of walking guns, as of course many still do, but they also play a vital role at driven shoots, working in the beating line and hunting out game for standing guns. Their secondary function is as retrievers, though there are plenty of spaniels which are kept primarily, or even solely, to fulfil the retrieving role. Pickers-up, driven game shooters, pigeon shooters and wildfowlers all use spaniels as retrieving dogs rather than as hunters of live game, and in this the spaniel breeds are something of a mirror image of the retrievers where dogs whose primary role is retrieving are used to hunt and flush.

As we have seen, the classification of spaniels as 'Springers' was a somewhat hit and miss affair during the nineteenth century. Certainly the Boughey family records establish their Springer lines from the very early years of the eighteenth century right through to the nineteen-thirties, and as far back as 1570 Dr Caius was using the term 'springer' to describe 'spaniells' which 'sprang' their game (i.e. flushed it), but there was no clear-cut division between Springers and Cockers. The Springer was a large working spaniel, the Cocker a small one, with the dividing line somewhere about the two stone mark. Gervase Markham wrote a book called *Hunger's Prevention or the Whole Art of Fowling by Land and Water*, published in 1655, in which he divided the land spaniels into two categories – the Crouching Spaniel (which is the ancestor of today's setters) and the Springing Spaniel. The Springing Spaniels were further sub-divided with a smaller variety being named the Cocking Spaniels, though it was clear that both came from the same stock and were not separate breeds. They are now, of course, two distinct breeds, and there is not, or should not be, any inter-mixing of bloodlines between the two if the progeny are to be considered pure-bred. Springer/Cocker crosses are, in fact, quite popular with some sportsmen, and are usually called Sprockers, though this is not a breed which the Kennel Club recognises. I suppose they could equally well have been labelled 'Cringers', though this hardly describes the proper demeanour of a working spaniel.

At the beginning of this century the introduction of field trials for spaniels saw the Springer begin to consolidate its popularity, and the English Springer Spaniel Club was formed in 1921. Early breeders of Springers worked, trialled and showed their dogs, but since those days there has been a complete divergence of type between the show and working strains of Springer. The show dog of today is certainly an elegant and handsome animal, and can make an excellent family pet as well, but ninety years of show breeding have almost totally eroded the working instincts which should be fundamental to the breed. By the same token, the working dogs bear little resemblance to the show specimens, so there is no point in buying a working-bred Springer if you have ambitions in the direction of the show ring.

It is as a hunting dog that the Springer is seen at its best, a job that was well summarised by Teasdale-Buckell: 'The principal requirement in the hunting spaniel is nose, quickness, never going out of gunshot, instant obedience, and bustling up game in a hurry without chasing it when it is up, dropping to shot, and retrieving dead and wounded game when told. It is a large order, and yet dogs that can do it all often make no more than £15 at auction, and sometimes less.' Compare that with the prices that were paid for pointers and setters at that time, when £100 was commonplace and £1,000 was by no means unknown. Indeed, Champion Lang was priced at 5,000 guineas at the Crystal Palace show in 1875, and it hardly bears thinking how much that represents at today's inflationary values.

The Springer is perhaps at his best when used as a roughshooter's dog, hunting always within gunshot of his master and flushing the quarry for the gun. There is a similar pleasure in watching a good Springer hustling and bustling, stern wagging and nose hoovering, to following a team of pointers on the open hill, and for some sportsmen the dogwork is more important than the actual shooting itself. A good Springer needs a high degree of courage where thorns and brambles, nettles and gorse bushes have to be hunted out, and hunted out properly, and cuts, scratches and stings are taken as a matter of course.

The practice of docking spaniels, and other breeds, has been the subject of a great deal of controversy recently, with new legislation which effectively banned docking, with the exception of working dogs, and banned anyone other than a veterinary surgeon from performing the operation. The result has been that many spaniels will have to work with full tails in the future. The reason for docking working spaniels was to prevent them from injuring the tips of their tails when they were working in thick cover. The reason for docking pet and show dogs was because certain breeds were normally docked. In future many working spaniels will be left with full tails, and it remains to be seen whether the predicted damage will result. It has been argued by some commentators that foxhounds are also expected to work in thick cover, and are left with full tails; by others that it is a far more cruel practice to leave a working dog with a full tail and expose it to injury than to subject it to a moment of pain when it is just a few days old. Logic suggests that both parties cannot be right, but I have not seen enough undocked spaniels working to say with authority that they will, or will not, suffer as a result.

Unless a Springer is used exclusively in the beating line it will almost certainly be required to retrieve as well as to flush game. This has been a part of their work since their first use to flush game for the gun, though when the quarry was netted, coursed or taken with hawks the spaniel's task would have been completed at the moment of the flush – much the same as a pointer or setter's task is often said to be finished today. Many working spaniels, though, are used mainly, or solely, as retrievers. They are popular as non-slip retrievers with many driven shots, as picking-up dogs, and as wildfowlers' and pigeon shooters' dogs, all occupations in which the dog is not required until after the game has been shot. Since the Springer, by its very name, is a dog which was bred to flush rather than to gather its quarry it might seem illogical to use one to do the work for which specialist retrieving breeds have been developed, but in practice there is no reason why a Springer, properly trained, should not make an adequate, and even an excellent, retriever.

Many are asked, and expected, to work at times as hunting and flushing dogs and at other times as non-slip retrievers, and there are plenty of Springers around that can do both jobs to a very high standard. There are not a few around that perform both jobs to a deplorably low standard, but that is almost certainly the fault of the handlers and trainers rather than of the dogs themselves. A Springer needs a lot of energy and a lot of stamina to put in a full day's work in thick cover, and it is necessary that that energy be properly controlled and channelled. The dog must work for you, not for itself, or certainly not for itself at the expense of your own requirements. Some can be very reliable and responsive, once their training is complete, but there are also plenty of Springers which must have firm handling if they are not to become the dominant partner.

The Cocker Spaniel

The subject of firm handling makes this an appropriate time to consider the Cocker Spaniel. As we have seen earlier, the dividing line between Cockers and Springers was at one time nothing more than a mark on a set of scales, though it should not be inferred that the modern Cocker Spaniel is no more than an undersized Springer. There are several substantial differences, not only in their size but in their temperament, methods of working and general attitude to life as well.

As we have already seen, the Cocker and the Springer are closely related, sharing common ancestors as recently as the early years of the present century. It might seem logical that there would be more similarities than differences between the two breeds, but in practice typical dogs of each breed are distinctly different. True, there are those Cockers which work like a Springer, and there are some Springers which work like Cockers; and depending on which breed you favour you may consider either or both parts of that statement to be an insult to that breed. Or perhaps a compliment.

The typical Cocker though is quite definitely a different dog to his larger cousin. The name 'Cocker' is believed by some to be a corruption of 'woodcock', and thus to point to the original use of the Cocker Spaniel, which was to hunt woodcock. There are contemporary records of spaniels being used in Wales to flush woodcock into nets, and it is possible that these 'Cocking' spaniels have direct links to the modern Cocker, though there have certainly been infusions of blood from many other sources as well.

The Cocker comes in a whole range of colours: solid black, liver or gold, liver and white, black and white, blue roan and red roan, and possibly some others that I have overlooked. Indeed, I was recently very tempted by a delightful little Cocker which was picking up at a driven grouse shoot, and only a chronic lack of pennies stopped me from making an offer for him. He was a solid chocolate shade, and most appropriately called Cadbury. Colour is really only relevant as far as seeing the dog in thick cover is concerned, though it might be worth considering that a dog with a proportion of white is usually easier to see than a whole coloured, darker animal.

The small size of the Cocker when compared to the other spaniel breeds is often cited by the breed's detractors – and there are a few – as evidence that the little dogs cannot be as useful as their own favourite breeds. 'A good big 'un will always beat a good little 'un' is a familiar argument, but not one that will hold up under close inspection. A fit working Cocker is quite capable of retrieving almost anything that you are likely to shoot over a spaniel. True, he might struggle over, say, a Canada goose, but the Cocker is not the dog you need if goose shooting is your game. Stick to proper spaniel work though and the Cocker will cope quite adequately, up to and including hares. Indeed it is as a rabbit dog that the little Cocker is seen at his best, and the breed probably suffered more than any other when the rabbit population was devastated by myxomatosis in the mid-fifties. Cockers like to work where they know there is game. That may sound a statement of the obvious, so I will qualify it. A Springer, presented with an area of cover and invited to 'get on', will happily bash his way through it in the hope that there might be rabbit or pheasant concealed therein. In contrast the Cocker is more inclined to stir himself into action if his nose tells him that there is a rabbit or pheasant in the vicinity, or that there has been one in the not too distant past.

They have a reputation for being possessed of an evil sense of humour; indeed, that great trainer and handler of Cocker Spaniels, Keith Erlandson, has suggested that they are possessed of the Devil himself. I have never found any reason to disagree with that viewpoint. The working Cocker can certainly be a mischievous little brute, and you may well find a stronger adjective than 'mischievous' springing to mind at times. They are not particularly 'hard' dogs as such, and the most effective answer to a recalcitrant Cocker is unlikely to be a stroke from an ash plant. Corporal punishment may well result in a dog which refuses to co-operate at all in the future.

That said, with Cockers, as with any breed of gundog, it is essential that you know the dog before you begin training. Some must have sensitive handling; some can be chastised quite effectively with nothing more than a raised voice. You have to assess each dog individually and act accordingly.

Cockers certainly have an evil side to their nature, but they can be sensitive as well, and the two characteristics are not mutually exclusive in any one dog. Think of it as a challenge.

Even more than the Springer, the Cocker is at his best when he is hunting for live game, preferably in a place where there is plenty of it. They are not the ideal choice for the man who wants a retrieving dog to sit beside his peg at a driven shoot, though there are Cockers which do just that and do it well. If you already have a Cocker and want to use it as a retriever as well as in its proper role of a hunting dog, then there is no law which says you cannot. On the other hand, if you are considering which dog you should get to use as a non-slip retriever then I would not suggest that the Cocker should feature too highly on your list. If, though, you enjoy rabbit shooting, and have access to ground with a plentitude of rabbits, or some rough ground where you can hunt pheasant and woodcock, and you take as much pleasure in seeing dog work as you do in the actual shooting, then a Cocker may well be the ideal choice for you. A Springer enthusiast could no doubt make a good case for getting a Springer rather than a Cocker, but there is one overriding argument that will cancel out all the cold logic that such an enthusiast may bring to bear on the subject. You may simply want a Cocker Spaniel, and prefer the little Cocker to all the larger alternatives. And if you do, and you can find a good little 'un, then you will have a dog that can do pretty much anything you might ask of it. Provided, of course, that it decides to co-operate.

The Springer and the Cocker are by far and away the most commonly seen of the working spaniels, the other breeds all being somewhat rare in the shooting field. Nevertheless, there are working strains of all the breeds, and it is possible, though it may not be easy, for the shooting man who has a particular desire for a Clumber, Sussex or Field Spaniel, for example, to obtain a pup which has the right background to equip it for work.

The Welsh Springer Spaniel

It is quite likely that the Welsh Springer has much the same background as the Cocker Spaniel, and that the Welsh Springers of today are directly related to those early hunting dogs which flushed woodcock into the huntsmen's nets. Those early spaniels were described as red and white dogs and the Welsh Springer of today is also invariably coloured red and white. Enthusiasts for the breed claim that they are the most ancient of the spaniel breeds, and that their lineage has remained pure right back to the Middle Ages.

They are larger than the Cocker but slightly smaller than the Springer and are undeniably one of the best looking of the gundog breeds.

Although their lineage is ancient they were only recognised as a separate breed by the Kennel Club in 1902, before which they were sometimes registered as Cockers, and in some cases the offspring of these 'Cockers' were registered as Springers. The First World War saw a dramatic decline in their numbers, a decline which was reversed to some extent until the Second World War dealt the breed another setback from which it has never really recovered.

The Welsh Springer has something of the look of the Brittany Spaniel about it (or perhaps I should say the Brittany has the look of a Welsh Springer), and there is some evidence that there may have been a mixing of bloodlines between the two breeds. Their colour and their small ears help to distinguish them from the Springer, and Springer devotees might add 'their working ability' (or lack of it) to those points. This is not entirely because they have been bred largely for show, or as pets, in recent years, but also because of their different style of working. They tend to be steadier than the English Springer, and this may be criticised as a lack of pace by observers used to the bustle of the larger dog. They are, like the Cocker, less inclined to exert themselves unduly in the absence of scent, and usually need more sensitive training and handling than the English Springer.

Retrieving is not always their strong point, though they normally have good, soft mouths. They were often worked as a team in times past, three, four or five Welsh Springers being used to beat through a covert and flush game which was then collected by retrievers, and this may have led to a diminution of the importance of retrieving instinct when their owners were selecting breeding stock. Their ability in teamwork was evidenced by the success of Mr A. T. Williams' Welsh Springers in the Spaniel Field Trials Team Stakes of 1900, 1901 and 1904.

Despite this you may be wondering why anyone should consider a Welsh Springer as a worker when there are English Springers and Cockers available. There is, of course, another side to the argument. Those owners of working Welsh Springers that I have met and talked with all maintain that they would not exchange their little red and white dogs for any other breed, no matter what advantages the English Springers and Cockers might appear to enjoy in theory. And if you can pronounce yourself fully satisfied with your dog, and really mean it, then why should you consider swapping it for anything else?

The Clumber Spaniel

The Clumber is quite distinctive in appearance; unmistakably a spaniel, but a far slower and heavier dog than any of the other varieties. They are not only bigger bodied; their heads are broad and square with deep lips and heavy muzzles, and they are predominantly white in colour with lemon or orange markings.

Their early history is well documented. They take their name from Clumber Park in Nottinghamshire, the seat of the Dukes of Newcastle, where they were established as a breed at the end of the eighteenth century. It is said that they first came to the estate as a gift to the Duke of Newcastle from the Duc de Noailles, though some authorities have suggested that they might actually be descended from a now defunct variety known as the Blenheim Spaniel.

In the early years of spaniel field trials – 1900 to 1906 – Clumbers were one of the most successful breeds competing, but they were soon overtaken by the faster and more eye-catching Springers. C. A. Philips, writing in *Hounds and Dogs* (Lonsdale Library), says this of their early successes: 'As they were judged more on game-finding merits and less on style and pace than is sometimes the case now, it was very necessary that they should be good stayers.' This contrasts completely with the views of Stonehenge, writing of the Clumbers thirty years before those trials were held: 'It is not, however, a poor man's dog, as it soon tires, and less than two or three couple would be quite useless in any covert of average size.' Not a very complimentary view, though he does go on to say that '. . . their mute, steady, and quiet style of hunting make[s] them eminently useful'.

The Clumber is certainly a slower, more plodding dog than a hard-driving Springer or Cocker, and it is easy to see why, after those early years of success, they struggled to impress trial judges when running against the far more eye-catching style of the other spaniel varieties. Not every shooting man, nor indeed more than a small minority of shooting men, will ever run their spaniels in field trials, and for many a slower dog which is possibly more thorough in its hunting may be preferable to the more usual varieties.

It is said that, particularly on days when scent is poor, the pace, or lack of pace, of the Clumber Spaniel makes it less likely to miss game than any of the other spaniel breeds. They should be very bold in cover, attacking it in the manner of a tank, and bulldozing their way through, rather than insinuating themselves into it in the way of a Cocker, and they are generally fond of water. Being more laid back and placid than most of the other spaniels suits them to a role as non-slip retrievers, though they lack the almost obsessive desire to retrieve something, anything, that is found in the Labrador, and may require a careful introduction to this aspect of their work.

They are by no means everyone's idea of a working spaniel. If you are hooked on the flailing sterns and hustling, bustling style of a Springer or Cocker then you may find the steady plod of a Clumber not to be to your taste. Equally, if you value game-finding above pace and style, and are taken with the soulful, lugubrious expression of the Clumber, and have room in your house or kennel for eighty pounds or so of spaniel, then a Clumber might suit you very well. As with the other minor spaniel breeds you will need to look long and hard to be sure that you get a pup with real working ability, but there are some about. And unlike the owners of the ubiquitous black Labradors, you are not likely to have any trouble identifying 'your dog' in the course of a shooting day.

The Field Spaniel

As we have seen earlier, 'Field Spaniel' was used by Stonehenge as a collective term which distinguished the 'land' spaniels from the water spaniels. At the same time, though, Field Spaniels were being exhibited in shows, though the division of the Spaniel classes – under two stone was a Cocker, over two stone a Springer, unless it was solid coloured in which case it was a Field Spaniel – would have today's exhibitors scratching their heads and consulting the rule books, not to mention the pedigree forms.

Field Spaniels suffered greatly at the beginning of this century from attempts to cross the breed with various others, most disastrously with basset-hounds, to try and get longer backs. It has to be said that the experiment was successful, successful in producing a stumpy-legged, sway-backed, hairy caterpillar of an animal that was little or no use in the field. Better sense eventually prevailed though, and more judicious crossing produced the ancestors of the modern Field Spaniel, which is of course a breed in its own right rather than a collective term for other varieties.

Some of the early photographs of Field Spaniels, taken around the turn of the century, show the basset-hound influence very clearly, and it is not surprising that there was a lively, not to say acrimonious, debate between working gundog owners and the show breeders who were responsible for these abominations. The modern Field Spaniel is a much more workmanlike shape, and is one of the best looking of the spaniel breeds. The solid colouring which marked the early Field Spaniels apart from their Springer relations is still found, though in various shades besides the black which was the most common in the last century.

I have been most impressed by the character and the ability of the Field Spaniels which I have seen at work, and find it a little surprising that they are not more popular as working dogs than seems to be the case. They have the reputation of being easy to train, but also of having an independent side to their characters, though they are certainly not the only gundog at which that accusation could be levelled. While I can see little reason beyond the problem of finding a suitable puppy to suggest that the sporting shot should not avail himself of a Field Spaniel, neither can I suggest any overriding reason why the Field Spaniel should be preferred to a Springer or Cocker.

Of course, if you are already hooked on Field Spaniels, or you want something a little different from the normal run of working spaniels, then no further reason is required. And you will also be doing your bit towards preserving one of our rarer breeds and, assuming that you want to shoot over it, maintaining the tradition of work that goes back well over a hundred years.

The Sussex Spaniel

Like the Field Spaniel, the Sussex Spaniel suffered great indignities at the hands of show breeders at the beginning of the century. Bred with long backs and short legs, the show dogs were so far removed from the conformation needed to perform a job of work that they were effectively useless in the field.

Dedicated work by a handful of working gundog breeders has succeeded in preserving the Sussex despite two times of real crisis at the end of both world wars when the breed was almost extinct. In 1918 there were only five Sussex Spaniels registered, and again in 1945 the world population of the breed was down to eight dogs. In spite of this they have survived, if not prospered, and a few can still be found today, though you will have to look long and hard to find a good, working specimen.

Somewhere between a Clumber and a Field Spaniel in their conformation and style of work, they are noted for their thick, golden-liver coats which are generally described as having the texture of sealskin. Not surprisingly they are good in water, and have the reputation of being strong, hardy dogs with excellent stamina, good noses and a willingness to please their handlers that may not always be evident in some of the other spaniel breeds.

In contrast to most gundogs the Sussex is allowed to give tongue while working, something that would normally be considered a serious fault. Stonehenge, who was writing at a time when the Sussex was a common sight in the shooting field, had this to say of them:

'This spaniel is much faster in his work than the Clumber, and more lasting, by which qualities he recommends himself to the general shooter. A couple or leash will suffice for most people, and even a single dog will beat a great extent of covert, if he is a good one. He is gifted with a full bell-like tongue, which he varies according to the game before him; and by this means an experienced shooter can tell whether to expect "fur" or "feather", and can also distinguish a hot scent from a stale one, by which he is considerably benefited. There is no better "all-round" spaniel than this, and I am not surprised at the rise in fashion shown in his case of late years.'

With such a glowing reference it seems strange that the Sussex should have been relegated to an extremely minor position in the ranks of working gundogs in the hundred and something years since those words were written. Nonetheless, you will see very few of the breed working today, though there are still a few owners who work their dogs. Again, as with the Field Spaniel, it will not be easy to find a working dog if you decide that a Sussex is the dog for you.

The Irish Water Spaniel

It is debatable whether the Irish Water Spaniel really belongs in the spaniel section, or whether it should be classed as a retriever. The Kennel Club is of little help in this matter since Irish Water Spaniels are classed as 'Spaniels' for the purpose of the show ring, but compete in retriever trials rather than spaniel trials. And to confuse the matter further, they actually used to compete in spaniel trials until the mid-nineteen-eighties, when their classification was altered.

Stonehenge classed them as Water Spaniels – as distinct from 'Field Spaniels', by which he meant 'Land Spaniels' – and sub-divided the breed into the Southern Irish and the Northern Irish varieties, though he had little to say about the Northern version. The breed was seemingly going through a bit of a crisis at the time of his writing, and his remarks were all qualified by such phrases as 'According to trustworthy evidence . . .' and 'Those who have possessed a dog of this breed speak very highly of them . . .', so it seems likely that he had little first-hand knowledge of them himself.

The breed has ancient origins, and is mentioned in Shakespeare's *The Two Gentlemen of Verona*, when Launce says of his lady, 'She hath more qualities than a water spaniel / Which is much in a bare Christian . . .' Long before then, in a document of AD 17, there is mention of 'Spaniels' being supplied to the King in return for land in Ireland, and it is maintained by some authorities that these dogs would have been the forerunners of the Irish Water Spaniel. Suffice to say that the Irish Water Spaniel is undoubtedly an ancient breed with a lineage running back thousands rather than hundreds of years.

The Irish Water Spaniel is a most distinctive dog, and while he could be confused with the Curlycoated Retriever at first glance, there is no similarity between him and any of the other spaniel varieties. They have a thick, curly, brown coat which is almost waterproof, set off by the short hair on their faces and tails – some admirers call them 'rat-tailed retrievers' – and by their distinctive top-knot. Taller and more leggy than any other spaniel, they are superb in water and can easily deal with a goose, and were accepted as the wildfowlers' dog long before the arrival of the specialist retrievers. Sir Ralph Payne-Gallwey wrote in *Letters to young Shooters*: 'A good dog, a brown Irish Water Spaniel for choice, is indispensable.' Those who own and work these big, intelligent dogs today are unlikely to disagree with that.

They are still excellent dogs for the wildfowler, though this does not preclude their use both as conventional retrievers and for hunting game for the walking gun or in the beating line. Their coats do require more maintenance than, say, a Labrador's, and they can hardly be expected to get into thick cover with the same alacrity as a good Springer, but they can do the job if required. They have the reputation of being something of a 'one man', or perhaps 'one family', dog with a suspicion of strangers – not necessarily a fault – and are undoubtedly highly intelligent.

It is a little surprising that they are not more popular in the shooting field, though this may be linked to their having to compete in spaniel trials for the first eighty-five years of this century. While certainly capable of the sort of work required by spaniel judges, they were hardly likely to shine against the more specialist Springers. It will be interesting to see what impact they have now that they are grouped with the retrievers.

The Kooikerhondje

One other spaniel breed which has been imported to Britain recently is the Dutch Kooikerhondje (pronounced 'Koy-ker-hond-je'). The Kooiker is a very attractive little red and white spaniel, built almost along the lines of a miniature setter, with a white-plumed tail and distinctive black tips to the ears which are known as earrings. Many old Dutch paintings have a little red and white spaniel somewhere in the picture, and these are almost certainly Kooikerhondjes.

The main use for the Kooiker is as a decoy dog, running in and out of the blinds which screen off the edges of the pipes radiating out from the centre of a duck decoy. Twisting in and out of sight, the Kooiker would attract the attention of the ducks, whose curiosity would then cause them to swim up the pipe after the dog. A few years ago this would have had fatal consequences for the duck; nowadays they are more likely to find them-selves in a scientist's notebook than in a poultry market.

Spaniel Work

It is not a simple matter to define 'spaniel work'. There are two possible lines to pursue. We can consider the traditional view of the work of a spaniel – hunting and flushing game for the gun, the hawk, the greyhound, or for the bird-catcher's net – or we can look at the work which spaniels actually do, in the field, today.

The second option imposes very few limitations. Spaniels can be found on driven shoots, doing the work of the non-slip retriever and sitting patiently, or perhaps impatiently, beside their masters while others manoeuvre grouse, pheasant or partridge to fly within gunshot. They can be found in the beating line at those same shoots, doing the manoeuvring mentioned above, and they can be found back behind the guns, picking up. Indeed, they can be found anywhere that a retriever is required, from the grouse moor to the foreshore, the pigeon hide to the flight pond. They don't hold a point, usually, though many will point momentarily before flushing game, and can be encouraged to develop this instinct if you want a spaniel that points.

As retrievers they can work as well as any but the best of the specialist retrieving breeds, and will make up with courage and enthusiasm what they may lack in body size and length of leg. We are, of course, considering spaniels in general and not any breed of spaniel in particular. I am not suggesting for a moment that a Cocker would be the right dog to send across a swift-flowing river to retrieve a Canada goose, though I have little doubt that someone is going to write and tell me that they have a Cocker which does just that.

There has never been a clear distinction between flushing breeds and retrieving breeds, in that the spaniels will always have been expected to retrieve as well as to hunt out game for the guns, while the specialist retrievers were never really so 'specialised' that they were not considered capable of hunting for live quarry. Nowadays the roles of the flushing and the retrieving breeds have become interwoven to such an extent that many prospective 'retriever' owners will automatically plump for a spaniel, just as many a Labrador is trained specifically to work in the beating line, or to hunt game for a walking gun.

That said, the 'real' work of the spaniels, by which I mean their traditional role in the shooting field, is to hunt game in front of the guns, flush it to be shot, and finally retrieve it. Consider the words of Major Maurice Portal DSO, writing a chapter on field trials for the Lonsdale Library publication *Shooting by Moor, Field and Stream* (1929). He says:

'In judging it may perhaps be said that eighty per cent of good spaniel work lies in finding game and showing the desire to do so under all conditions which entail nose, brains, steadiness and control, while about twenty per cent of the value of the work done rests in style of work and the retrieve. A spaniel is expected to quarter its ground with method and to range within gunshot, to search out any thick clumps it may meet, whether old thorns or brambles, etc., to be steady to shot or wing, to push out a rabbit from its seat and not pounce on it, and not to run the line of one which has moved on.'

That passage was written some sixty-five years ago, but it still holds good. If you are using a spaniel to hunt up game for the gun, then the hunting and flushing side of the work is obviously far more important than the retrieving of the shot game. In saying that I am not intending to diminish the importance of finding any game that is shot, particularly if the quarry happens to be wounded, but rather attempting to stress the importance of the game-finding and game production in spaniel work.

If the dog fails to find game, and to produce it in such a manner that the gun can shoot it, then there will be no call for a retrieve. And when game is shot over a spaniel the retrieve will normally take place pretty much as soon as the bird falls, and should therefore be a relatively simple procedure when compared with, for example, a driven shoot where a great many birds may have to be collected, and a significant time may have passed between the fall of the bird and the signal for the dog to get on to collect it. This does not mean that retrieving is unimportant, nor that unsteadiness, hard mouth, poor marking or any of the other 'retriever' faults can happily be over-looked in the working spaniel. If my dog is unsteady to fall of game, chases fur, or is hardmouthed, then my dog is fundamentally flawed. True he may be brilliant at some other aspect of his work, but a fault is a fault is a fault, and no amount of glossing over it can disguise the fact.

However, looking at the matter from a practical shooting man's point of view, as opposed to that of a field trial enthusiast, we may be prepared to forgive some transgressions provided there is something to trade off in return. If your spaniel is going to be doing spaniel work *per se*, and if you are going to be shooting where game is not very plentiful, you may well feel that the most important thing that your dog has to do is to find whatever game there is, and get it flushed within gunshot. If he can't do that, then the question of quality in retrieving will never arise.

Major Portal was describing the qualities needed in field trial spaniels of the nineteen-twenties, but what he says holds good for the working spaniel of the present day. If the dog is to find what game there is then it is obviously essential that it hunts the ground methodically; if it quarters erratically, or just mills about aimlessly, then obviously game will be missed, and if it draws out of gunshot to flush game then chances will be lost. The courage to face thick cover is another vital aspect of spaniel work: if a rabbit or pheasant is determined to remain tucked into the middle of a bramble patch, then there it will remain unless your dog has the courage and determination to bore in there and force it out.

But let us assume that the bird or the rabbit has been forced out from its refuge, and that you have held straight. The retrieve is important, certainly, but I would suggest that the style and pace of the retrieve will be of less importance, to the average shooting man, than the fact that the quarry is collected, one way or another, and brought to the gamebag. Certainly it is a pleasure to watch a fast and stylish retrieve brought properly to hand, sitting delivery and all, but it isn't essential, unless you are running the dog in a competition.

Whatever you may have read into the above, please do not take me to task for advocating low standards in spaniel work. I am not. What I am saying, though, is that for the practical shot, out on a rough shoot with a spaniel, the most important part of the dog's work is to provide the means for the sport – to get game on the move in front of the guns. A lack of attention to the finer points of retrieving will not make a good game-finding dog into a bad dog, though one that can do both jobs to a high standard is obviously a better one.

Style of working is another area where the line between field trial dogs and 'shooting' dogs can be a little blurred. Trial judges are clearly looking for quality in the dog's work. The question is, will what a trial judge considers 'quality work' necessarily coincide with your own definition? The judge will probably be looking for a hard-going, pacy, stylish dog which is eye-catching and exciting to watch. You, on the other hand, may want something a little less thrusting, a little less pacy and perhaps a little bit easier to handle. A top trialling spaniel is sometimes a little bit like a Formula One racing car: very quick and very exciting, but too much of a handful for everyday use. And no, this is not a sideways swipe at field trial spaniels, just an observation that the type of hard-going, thrusting dog that wins trials may not be the ideal companion for every shooting man. You may want a gentler, slower dog that can be left to potter along all day with the minimum of handling. You may be quite content to proceed at a gentle amble while the dog makes good every bit of cover, at its own pace. And if that is what you want, then your ideal dog will not be the type that keeps the handler literally at the end of his whistle and metaphorically on the edge of his seat. I am not saying that a slower dog is better than a fast one, simply that different owners will have different requirements from their dogs, even though the dogs are doing the same work.

You may, of course, be a dedicated spaniel owner but not a dedicated rough shot; a wildfowler, perhaps, a pigeon decoyer, a picker-up, or simply a keen driven shot. Your spaniel may be first and foremost a retrieving dog, and if so, you may well put a greater emphasis on the retrieving side of spaniel work: the need to handle the dog to a particular spot where a fallen bird was marked; the ability of the dog to mark birds for itself; pace and style of retrieving; the nose to take the line of a runner and hunt it out through fresh scent and foiled ground. Or perhaps you are a beater and need, above all else, a dog which is calm and controllable when in close proximity to several (or several hundred) pheasants, milling about at a flushing point.

Whatever your requirement, a good spaniel of the right breeding can do it for you, provided it has had the right training and the right handling. As to which of the breeds is the right one for you, the logical answer is that, for most shooting men, either an English Springer or a Cocker represents the best and easiest chance of getting a dog with the right working background and the necessary ability to do your job for you. But that said, there is also an argument for all the other breeds: the Welsh Springer, the Irish Water Spaniel, the Clumber and the rest. The final decision is, of course, up to you.

The Hunt, Point and Retrieve Breeds

There is a tendency in Britain to regard the Hunt, Point and Retrieve breeds – HPRs for short – as relative newcomers to the shooting field, a view that only holds good if we are being insular, and referring solely to the shooting fields of Britain. Closer examination will reveal that, in their countries of origin, some of the 'newcomer' HPR breeds were actually established long before our own retrievers and spaniels were settled and standardised over here.

Although there were many changes in the way in which gundogs, and particularly the spaniels, were classified during the nineteenth and very early twentieth centuries, those changes were generally of the mix and match variety. Norfolk Spaniels came and went, the term Field Spaniel, once applied to a group of breeds, became the name of a specific breed of dog, and the various retrieving breeds were given stable classifications. There were, though, no new breeds introduced to the country until the late nineteen-forties, since when some nine or ten 'new' breeds have been introduced, most of which are Hunt, Point and Retrieve dogs.

The quarantine regulations, which made the importation of dogs a difficult and expensive business, were certainly partly responsible for the stagnation of the number of gundog varieties in Britain during the inter-war years. However, since the last war, despite those regulations remaining in force and being strictly enforced, our register of gundog breeds has grown, and is still growing. We have had German Short-haired Pointers, German Wirehaired Pointers, Weimaraners and Vizslas for many years; Large Musterlanders, Brittany Spaniels (the 'Spaniel' part of the name was dropped 'to avoid confusion with the spaniel breeds') and Italian Spinones have appeared more recently; there are a few Wirehaired Vizslas about, and no doubt other breeds will arrive in the future. All of the former are HPR breeds, and they represent by far the majority of the 'new' breeds. There are some others: Chesapeake Bay Retrievers, Nova Scotia Duck Tolling Retrievers and Kooikerhondjes are all here and growing in popularity, but their numbers are currently tiny in comparison with the HPRs. The latter two are also here primarily at the behest of dog show enthusiasts rather than by virtue of their abilities as working gundogs.

The first Pointer Retrievers were brought here at the end of the war by servicemen who had seen the dogs working on the Continent and decided to try them back at home. The German Shorthaired Pointer (GSP), Weimaraner and Vizsla were the main early introductions, and all were imported as working dogs, until with Kennel Club recognition they became eligible to compete in field trials and in the show ring. Initially they took part in pointer and setter trials, but these were inadequate as a test of Pointer Retrievers, since they do not include a retrieving phase. The first trial for Pointer Retrievers was held in 1954, and in 1962 the Kennel Club awarded Field Trial Championship status to the HPR breeds.

It is to the enormous credit of the breeders of the various HPR varieties that they have been determined not to fall into the trap which has so debased many of the 'native' gundogs and allow their breeds to split into 'show' and 'working' strains. The average working English Setter or Cocker Spaniel has about as much chance of taking a Challenge Certificate at a Championship Show as it has of becoming the next Prime Minister. This is approximately equal to the chances of a Show Champion of either breed winning a field trial, and the same would apply to most, though not all, of the other 'native' gundogs. We, or our ancestors, have allowed many of our gundog breeds to split into two distinctive types, and there is little or no chance that the two strains will ever rejoin.

Depending on your allegiance, you may be saddened by the sight of working dogs that bear little resemblance to the accepted breed standard, or feel sorry for show dogs that are physically and mentally incapable of doing the work for which their breed was developed. There are a few individuals, in all breeds, who are trying to produce good-looking dogs which can do a proper day's work, and in some breeds they are quite successful. Perhaps if more working owners visited dog shows, and more show owners took up shooting, there might be some progress – but I rather doubt it will happen.

In the HPR breeds, though, a far healthier situation prevails. There are any number of working and trialling dogs that compete and win in the show ring. There are plenty of show dogs which can and do perform to a very high standard in the shooting field. Many breeders and owners would be insulted to be asked whether their dogs were show strain or working strain, since they simply breed working dogs of the correct type and temperament. The only sad thing about this is that, such is the state of some of our 'own' gundog breeds, it is relevant to comment on it at all.

The division of our traditional British breeds into show and working varieties took place long, long before most of the current breeders and exhibitors were born. As early as 1907 Mr Teasdale-Buckell was deploring the damage done to the working ability of gundogs by breeding solely for show, and the divisions have widened ever since to the point at which they are probably irreconcilable. Too many – far, far too many – gundogs are bred, exhibited and sold by owners who have no interest whatsoever in them as gundogs. They are bred for looks alone with no regard to those qualities which were the original *raison d'être* of the breed. It is at times depressing to see dogs which would quite patently be incapable of doing the job for which they were intended, being 'put up' by judges who clearly have no real concept of what a working gundog is all about.

But let us return to the HPR breeds. Perhaps because their owners had before them the example of what a hundred years of breeding for looks alone could do to working breeds they have managed to prevent their dogs dividing into 'showing' and 'working' types. For this I have nothing but praise. There is no requirement for a field trial entrant to conform to the breed standard, nor is there any suggestion that a show dog must have experience in the field, but it is good to know that both are distinct possibilities among the Hunt, Point Retrievers.

Any discussion of Pointer Retrievers must confront the prejudice that exists against the breeds in some shooting and field trialling quarters. Enthusiasts for the breeds can be quite outspoken in their praise for their dogs' ability; detractors can be equally forthright in condemning all HPRs as overrated pretenders to the rightful position occupied by our 'native' breeds. Depending on the authority, you may learn that Pointer Retrievers are the best gundogs in the country, or the worst; the answer to a shooting man's prayer or the substance of his worst nightmares. Let us try to distinguish fact from fantasy. Although they are clumped together under the blanket classification of 'Hunt, Point and Retrieve Breeds' it is important to appreciate that the different breeds are, well, different. A Vizsla is a quite different dog, physically as well as temperamentally, from a German Shorthaired Pointer, just as a Spinone differs from a Weimaraner or a Brittany. What they have in common though is the fact that all are Pointer Retrievers; not flushing dogs, not non-slip retrieving dogs, but pointing dogs which retrieve.

In the United States the breeds are grouped as Versatile Hunting Dogs, which description seems to me to be a pretty fair analysis of what they should be: versatile. Able to work grouse on the hill or pheasant in a low ground covert; retrieve duck from the flight pond, point partridge on an autumn stubble or track a wounded deer on the hill or in woodland. If you are fortunate enough to include some or all of the above in your shooting calendar, and you want one dog that can work on every occasion, then an HPR may well be just what you require. Let us consider the choices available to you.

The German Shorthaired Pointer

By far the most numerous of the working Hunt, Point Retrievers is the German Shorthaired Pointer. The Weimaraner may lead it in terms of the number of dogs registered with the Kennel Club, but at field trials and in the shooting field the GSP leads all the rest by a country mile.

The GSP may be the most popular dog among the enthusiasts for the HPR breeds, but it is also the breed which is most put down by the HPR detractors. Hard mouth and stubbornness are the general traits most often selected for criticism, and it cannot be denied that some German Pointers are indeed hardmouthed and/or stubborn. But so are some Labradors, some Golden Retrievers, some Cockers, some English Springers, and so on. There are good dogs and bad dogs in every breed and it is all too easy to condemn the whole of a breed because of the actions of a single individual. German Shorthaired Pointers are not all hardmouthed, nor are they all intractable, untrainable beasts. Indeed, they can have as soft a mouth as any Labrador, and the gentle temperament of a Lady's lapdog. Sometimes. And sometimes they certainly can be stubborn. As for the question of hard mouth? I don't believe any statistics are compiled relating to the reasons why dogs are eliminated from field trial stakes, but it would certainly be interesting reading if they were. I have attended several HPR stakes at which the main reason for elimination of the dogs (which were nearly all GSPs) was hard mouth. What I do not know is whether this is typical of all HPR stakes (and I doubt that it is), or what proportion of dogs in spaniel or retriever trials is eliminated for the same reason. I cannot, therefore, produce any real evidence to prove it, but I would suggest that hard mouth is probably rather more prevalent among German Shorthaired Pointers than it is among Labradors, Golden Retrievers, Flatcoats and the like. As to whether that constitutes grounds for you not purchasing a GSP only you can decide. Certainly, I would advise you to be wary if you were wanting your GSP solely for retrieving purposes, but if you want a dog solely for retrieving then why would you choose a Hunt, Point Retriever?

The German Shorthaired Pointer was first registered with the German Kennel Club in 1872, the honour of being the first in the book going to a dog called Hektor. The breed was originally developed from a cross between the Spanish Pointer and the Hanoverian Schweisshund, which produced a large, heavy dog called a German Pointer. Further crosses with (English) Pointers – which were themselves a mixture of Spanish Pointer, Foxhound etc. – changed the German Pointer into a lighter and faster dog which became known as the German Shorthaired Pointer. The modern German Shorthaired Pointer should be a strong, athletic dog, rather more heavily built than the British pointers and setters, though clearly of the same family. They are usually liver and white or black and white, though solid liver and solid black dogs can occur, and in my opinion look quite striking, though they are not popular with all GSP devotees. Their tails were always docked, though not to such a short length as were the spaniels', but this will probably become less common following the recent legislation on the subject.

The breed was specifically developed in order to carry out a very wide range of working activities. These include pointing game using air scent, hunting out game by foot scent, retrieving from land and water and tracking wounded game such as boar and deer. In Britain there was a tendency to develop specialist breeds for each type of work – retrievers, flushing spaniels, pointers and setters – whereas in Germany the effort was devoted to producing a single dog that could combine the work of all three. Inevitably there had to be compromises.

The retrievers are generally big, strong and relatively placid dogs; they need strength to carry game, patience to sit by a peg, thick coats to protect them when working in cold water and noses attuned to finding dead and wounded game. Spaniels are generally smaller, livelier, and longer coated to suit them for hunting through thick cover all day long. Pointers and setters are long and lean with superb air-scenting noses, equipped to run prodigious distances and take their birds from well back so as not to flush them prematurely. Obviously, it is not possible to combine all these sometimes incompatible qualities in a single dog.

Nevertheless, the German Shorthaired Pointer represents a pretty good attempt at so doing. A good GSP will cover a lot of ground, at a good pace, can point as staunchly as the next dog, will retrieve whatever he may be required to retrieve, can track wounded deer if required and will hunt thick cover like a spaniel. There are only two caveats that I must draw to your attention at this juncture. Firstly, it is hardly fair to expect a dog which is capable of such a range of tasks to carry them all out with the same aptitude as each of the specialist breeds, when engaged in its own speciality. Secondly, to train a GSP properly – that is, to train it to carry out all its various tasks and to carry them out to a high standard – is necessarily a longer and more difficult job than training a pointer which may not be required to retrieve, a spaniel which will never have to range out of gunshot, or a retriever which is not going to hunt live game.

It is a combination of those last two points which I believe has led to much of the flak which has buzzed around the heads of GSPs and their owners. Pointer and setter handlers judge the German dogs as if they were specialist bird-dogs; retriever trainers look for the same standard of work that a Labrador or Flatcoat should produce, and spaniel enthusiasts expected them to work cover like a good Springer. If they failed to match the very high standards of which each of the specialist breeds are capable, then they were condemned as 'useless foreign brutes'. Not a fair judgement, but one that has tended to stick.

There are few enough trainers and handlers who can get the best out of a gundog, any gundog, and more than enough of us who can take a potentially good puppy and turn it into something that does a job, but is still a long way from its true potential. More often than not this is our own fault, because we mucked up the training of the dog, or introduced it to the shooting field before it was ready. There is nothing intrinsically difficult about training the average gundog, but even so, plenty of us manage to make a Horlicks of it. Training an HPR to work properly is harder, simply because there is much more to cover. And of course, the act of purchasing a Pointer Retriever simply means that you will have more work to do in order to train it properly. It does not make you a more capable trainer.

Add our native conservatism and a touch of xenophobia, and it is easy to see why the HPR breeds are sometimes castigated, often with little real cause. Finally, the enthusiasm of some HPR owners may lead them to draw very unfavourable comparisons between their breeds and the older established 'British' breeds. This is never going to be good public relations for the HPRs. If you happen to have a really good working GSP, Vizsla or Brittany, its work will speak for itself. If it isn't a good 'un then nothing you say will convince me that it is.

The GSP is, as I have said, by far the most popular of the HPR breeds for use as a working dog. In much the same way as the Labrador and English Springer dominate their respective classifications, the German Shorthaired Pointer leads the HPR group. Part of this may be due to the availability of dogs, but it is probably fair to say that, certainly until quite recently, the British GSPs had an edge in working and field trialling ability over the other Hunt, Point Retrievers. This situation may alter with the introduction of more HPR breeds, though it will take a long time for one of the newer introductions to oust the GSP from its current position.

Hunting thick cover for rabbit or pheasant requires a dog with the courage to force its way among thorns and brambles, and the persistence to work out game which is reluctant to flush. On the open hill, where grouse are thinly spread, a dog must be able to get out and cover a lot of ground, and cover it systematically, have a nose that can find birds by air scent and be a staunch enough pointer to hold those birds until the guns have toiled their way across to him. A good GSP should be able to tackle either job, and tackle it to a decent standard, provided that it has had the necessary training and experience. It is hardly fair to take a dog which has worked all its life in small fields and woods and expect it to take immediately to quartering several hundred yards on either side of its handler, and covering hundreds of acres for every find. No more can you expect an experienced grouse dog to adapt at once to the more confined work needed on a well stocked pheasant shoot. Given the right experience, though, a GSP can, and many of them do, adapt to both types of work.

The German Wirehaired Pointer

At first glance the German Wirehaired Pointer may look like nothing more than a hairy version of the GSP, but this is not the case. The GWP is very much a breed in its own right. The first examples were brought to Britain just after the war, but the bloodlines were mixed with German Shorthaired Pointers, the results still being seen today in occasional throwbacks among German Wirehaired Pointer litters. A later introduction in the early seventies was managed more carefully, and the GWP is now beginning to gain acceptance both as a shooting dog and in the field trial arena.

With their dense, wiry coat they are perhaps better suited than the thinner coated GSP when confronting thick cover or working in cold water. The coat should be harsh to the touch, wiry even, with a thick undercoat beneath the wiry guard hairs to provide insulation and protection against thorn or bramble. Bushy eyebrows and a prominent moustache and beard lend the breed a distinctive and, to me, very appealing appearance and, like the GSP, their tails were normally docked.

As a breed the German Wirehaired Pointer is sometimes accused of being inclined to sharpness, and this is certainly true of some individuals, though many have excellent temperaments. In their native Germany the breed is used to track wounded boar and must of necessity be able to look after itself. The stubbornness and bravery required for this and the drive and determination needed by any wide-ranging hunting dog can cause problems in dogs which are kept solely as pets or for show and which lack the discipline and the outlet for their energies provided by shooting, and it may manifest as aggressive behaviour.

The GWP made an uncertain start to its time in Britain, not helped by the sheer lack of dogs which led to cross-breeding with the German Shorthaired Pointer. Now that they are firmly established and making their mark at trials as well as in the shooting field, it is likely that more of these strong, handsome dogs will be seen at work and in competition. Whether they will then begin to challenge the position of their shorthaired cousins remains to be seen, but for the shooting man who combines wildfowling with rough shooting the German Wirehaired Pointer is certainly a breed worthy of consideration.

The Hungarian Vizsla

The handsome, russet-gold Vizsla has an ancestry which goes back around a thousand years to a time when hunting dogs were brought to Hungary by invading Magyar tribesmen. These yellow coloured pointing dogs were crossed with the native Hungarian foxhound or Pannonian hound and gradually evolved into the distinctive dog that we know today. The name Vizsla is generally held to come from a village in the Danube valley, though I have also seen it linked to a Turkish word meaning 'to seek'.

Whatever the origin of the breed and its name, it is certain that the Vizsla was developed by the Hungarian aristocracy, originally to find game for their falcons, and later to hunt for the gun – a development that parallels that of most of the pointing breeds, whatever their country of origin. As shooting took precedence over falconry various other bloodlines were brought in to the breed, including Irish Setters and possibly blood-hounds. The first stud book specifically for the breed was begun in 1880.

Hungary is a country with vast, open tracts of plain and there is an obvious requirement for a dog that can get out and range widely to find the partridges, pheasants and hares which live there. And as with any wide-ranging gundog, it must then be able to point, and hold its quarry until the guns can come up within range. These requirements alone determine much about the conformation of the Vizsla: it has to be a long-legged, athletic dog with the speed and stamina to cover a lot of ground and the strength to retrieve heavy game such as hares. Add a requirement to work in water, and to stand the freezing winters of central Europe, and it is clear that the Vizsla needs a thick, water-resistant coat. Finally, the need to tackle wild boar and wolf meant a dog with strength and courage and a little more weight than was necessary in the British pointers and setters.

And so the Vizsla was developed. Their red-gold coat feels almost greasy to the touch, and all the Vizslas that I have known have shown a tremendous affinity for water. Their temperament is much softer than that of the GSP or GWP, yet there is still a steely determination to protect its own, including those humans it sees as part of its pack. Soft they may be to those they count as friends, but they will not hesitate to stand up to anyone they feel is threatening them, or their 'family', whether canine or human.

This softness and willingness to please calls for a different approach to training from that which may suit most other HPRs. Praise is generally more effective than punishment, and they are blessed – cursed? – with a sense of humour that can be infuriating at times, though it can be hilarious. I wonder if this harks back to their Irish Setter ancestry, since we have an Irish Setter dog at the moment who delights in playing tricks on 'his' humans, very much in the manner of some Vizslas. Do not be misled by my remarks about 'softness' and 'willingness to please' into thinking that training a Vizsla is a simple matter compared to training, say, a German Shorthaired Pointer. There is also a certain stubbornness and a willingness to do things their own way at times which can make life frustrating for the would-be trainer. Harsh words and punishment are unlikely to yield good results though, and it may be best simply to stop the lesson and wait until a more suitable mood takes over both you and your dog.

They are extremely affectionate, and need affection in return and have thus become very popular as pets as well as show dogs. Since the Vizsla is lacking the natural aggression of some of the other HPR breeds, breeding for show purposes can sometimes result in dogs which, although possessed of the physical attributes required, do not have the drive needed to get out and hunt properly. Remembering the Vizsla, perhaps more than any of the other HPR dogs, was bred specifically to quarter wide open spaces, it is disappointing to see dogs which are content to simply potter around under their handler's feet. Sadly, this lack of drive is not uncommon among some bloodlines, and the prospective owner should take care that a dog intended for work really does come from working stock.

They are usually excellent retrievers, being invariably softmouthed, and possessed of rather more patience than most pointing dogs when asked to sit quietly at a peg or in a butt. If they locate game which they are unable to collect they will sometimes stand by it and bay loudly and persistently, as I once discovered when picking up at a driven pheasant shoot. I had sent a Vizsla for a hit bird which had fallen in among a thick stand of pine trees, and was rewarded a few moments later by an awful, howling altercation from within the trees. Fearing that he had injured himself I ran across to the wood, only to find him staring up into the branches where, twenty feet above him, a wounded cock pheasant clung defiantly to a Scots pine. Whether he had found it by sight or scent I cannot say, but it required either good eyesight or an excellent nose to have done so.

If you find a Vizsla with the right drive and the correct conformation it can make an excellent grouse dog, and I have seen Vizslas in Sutherland which quartered the hill with all the pace and style of a good going pointer or setter, and were excellent bird-finders into the bargain. As for low ground partridge hunting, it is what the breed was developed to do, and they can still do it to a high standard, as well as working as retrievers and general purpose game-finders around the shoot.

I will freely admit to having a very soft spot for Vizslas, more because of their temperament than because they have any particular superiority as working dogs. If you want one of the Hunt, Point and Retrieve breeds to double as a working dog and a house dog, then one of these handsome and friendly Hungarians could be just the thing for you. Handled sensitively they make devoted and loyal companions as well as being capable and stylish workers, but the key words are 'handled sensitively'. If your training methods rely on dominating rather than coercing your pupils, then you might be better to think again.

The Weimaraner

Like the Vizsla, the Weimaraner has a well documented history going back to the days before the introduction of the gun into the sporting field. The breed originated in the Weimar Republic from which they derive their name, and was developed from the dogs which hunted in packs for larger game including boar, deer and possibly bear. As the development of the sporting gun made wing shooting possible so they were bred to find and point game for their handlers, and the subsequent refinements to the hunting dogs eventually resulted in the Weimaraner we know today.

The Grand Duke Karl August of Sax-Weimar-Eisenbach is known to have developed the working ability of the breed during the latter part of the eighteenth and early nineteenth centuries. The Weimaraner Club of Germany was formed in 1897 and jealously protected the breed for many years, regulating both the breeding and the ownership of the dogs. After the Second World War, though, the Weimaraner spread to Britain and to North America, and became, and is still, one of the most popular of the Hunt, Point and Retrieve breeds. In Britain they are probably the most numerous of the HPR dogs. However, popular though they are as pets, and in the show ring, they are far from common in the shooting field, and lag way behind the GSP in their participation, and success, in field trials.

To some extent their very striking appearance has acted against them. With their lean, athletic build and beautiful silver grey, almost metallic coat, they enjoy great popularity among owners who keep them solely as show dogs. However, there are plenty of working Weimaraners around the country, though obviously the percentage of British Weimaraners which are active workers is far below that of the GSPs, GWPs or Vizslas.

Perhaps because of its very houndy ancestry the Weimaraner is a less stylish worker than some of the other HPRs, tending to a low head carriage and a shorter range than some of its more popular rivals, and being more inclined to work on foot scent than to work with a high head carriage and find game on air scent. This has certainly told against it in terms of field trial results in the past, though more recent Kennel Club regulations require trial judges to consider each breed in the context of the way that particular breed should work, rather than judging all the dogs in a stake against the same standard. This is not to suggest that a Weimaraner or an Italian Spinone will be judged less critically than a GSP or a Vizsla. However, if a dog has been bred to work to a steady and thorough pattern of hunting then it is not realistic to expect it to raise its pace and change its style of work simply to try and compete with another breed which was originally developed to handle different terrain, and possibly different game. In pointer and setter field trials the modern Gordon Setter is at least as fast and wide running as any Pointer, English Setter or Irish Setter, and has to be in order to compete.

Top left: In wet conditions an Irish Setter will revel long after the thinner coated bird-dogs have given up.

Top right: A double 'sitting delivery' as the Labrador brings a grouse to her handler.

Above: A young Pointer, puzzled and slightly nervous at the click of the camera shutter.

Above left: Picking up with a Labrador after the drive while the guns are moving off to their next position.

Top right: Spring grouse counting with a Pointer; a useful time for training, and for running off the extra weight from a winter in the kennel.

Below right: Less common than its black cousins, this Yellow Labrador watches closely, ready to mark the fall.

Top left: Recovering after a run, this black Pointer shows clear signs of the greyhound blood which was introduced to the breed well over a hundred years ago.

Top right: Welsh Springer Spaniel taking a rest in the heather.

Above: Eager to please, these Hungarian Vizslas are typical of the breed in their steady concentration on their handler.

Above left: Safely to hand, a pheasant delivered to the handler by a German Shorthaired Pointer.

Top right: The gun watches closely as this German Shorthaired Pointer makes its way through thick cover to deliver a pheasant to its handler.

Above right: German Wirehaired Pointer collecting a hare.

Opposite: The rich chestnut and black marking of the Gordon Setter is well illustrated in this shot.

Top left: The bearded and whiskered German Wirehaired Pointer is better protected from cold and wet than the thin coated German Shorthair.

Top right: All Pointers are not hard-mouthed as can be seen from the lively attitude of this grouse, collected on a warm September day on the moors.

Above: Total concentration from this Irish Setter as it creeps forward ready to flush the grouse.

Opposite: If you have access to woodcock ground then there will be work for bird-dogs like this Pointer right through the shooting season.

This Hungarian Vizsla is rightly looking pleased with itself having just found, pointed and then produced a pheasant for the guns.

Whether substituting pace for stamina is real progress, or a retrograde step, is a matter of personal opinion, but it is clear that the modern field trialling Gordon Setter is a different dog to those that were considered to be the 'correct type' back in the nineteen-thirties.

The Weimaraner's more deliberate and persistent style of work may have been a handicap in competition, but it can also be a positive advantage to some owners who want a steady, persistent and less wide ranging dog than the general run of Hunt, Point Retrievers. They are probably not the best choice if you want a dog to hunt for grouse on the type of hill that has one barren pair per thousand acres, nor, with their relatively thin coats, are they suited as dogs for the coastal wildfowler. This is not to say that they won't find grouse, or retrieve duck; given the right handling and training they can do. However, if you want a dog primarily as a grouse finder or a water retriever then you would do well to look elsewhere.

But suppose you enjoy rough shooting, wandering around the shoot in the hope of a rabbit or two, the odd pheasant, perhaps a partridge or a woodcock. You shoot mostly alone, or perhaps with one companion. You might do some beating for a driven pheasant shoot, and decoy the odd pigeon. You want one dog that will come along whatever the occasion and do whatever is required. The birds on your shoot are a bit thinly spread for a spaniel to find, so a pointing dog might be a better bet, and you are not overly impressed by the sheer pace of the dog, provided that it finds what birds are there, and points them until you get to it. If that sounds like your sort of sport then a Weimaraner might well be the dog for you. I am not saying it is the only choice, or even the best choice, but it is a possibility that you might like to consider. The Weimaraner is a handsome and striking dog, and one that develops a deep loyalty to its owner, though this may also show in a certain amount of anti-social behaviour towards other people and dogs.

Like the GSP, the Weimaraner has a reputation for being hardmouthed, an accusation often lent weight by the assertion 'they have to kill cats and foxes in Germany'. There is some substance to the claim, but all Weimaraners are not hardmouthed cat-killers. It is true, though, that in Germany they are expected to deal with vermin, and to show some aptitude for guard dog work, and this should be borne in mind when considering buying one of the 'grey ghosts'. Only you know what your particular requirements of your dog may be, and it is quite possible that behaviour patterns that would put off another prospective owner would be the very ones that decide you to choose a Weimaraner.

The Brittany

The Brittany is a relative newcomer to Britain, having only arrived in the early nineteen-eighties, but it has quickly become familiar both at HPR Trials and in the shooting field. They were originally known as Brittany Spaniels, though the 'Spaniel' half of the name was quickly dropped, so that the dogs would not be confused with the spaniel breeds. It may appear a little strange that a dog such as the Brittany which is clearly and obviously a spaniel should be deprived of half its title, when the Irish Water Spaniel, which is now treated as a retriever rather than a spaniel, should retain the name. Certainly, the Brittany competes in HPR stakes rather than spaniel trials, but in France, and in Ireland, a Brittany Spaniel (or Epagneul Breton) it remains. What's in a name anyway?

I must further risk the wrath of Brittany owners when I attempt to describe the breed, since it is extremely hard to do so without using the 'S' word. There is an undoubted resemblance between the Brittany and the Welsh Springer, and given the close historical links between the two regions it is extremely likely that the breeds share common ancestors, if not a common designation. There is probably a certain amount of setter blood in the Brittany as well, introduced when British sportsmen took their dogs to Brittany, and possibly some influence of the Italian Braco and the Braque de Bourbonnais.

Whatever the origins, the breed today is a most attractive little dog looking like a rather long-legged spaniel both in conformation and coat, which is usually a combination of orange and white, black and white or liver and white, with some tricoloured dogs and some which are roan. In France their ancestors were known as *les fougères*, which means 'high-spirited', and for once I am fully in accord with our Gallic neighbours. High-spirited is a label that fits the Brittany like a surgeon's glove. I have heard a number of other labels applied to Brittanys, of which 'stubborn little brutes' is one of the more common, and more polite. Imagine a dog with all the eagerness and desire to hunt of a good spaniel, coupled with the pace and wide ranging habits of a setter, and you will have an idea of what the Brittany is all about. They may look like a long-legged spaniel, but they are quite definitely a pointing breed, and the whole idea of being a pointing dog is to operate out of range of the gun.

A good going Brittany is an absolute delight to watch working, combining pace, drive and enthusiasm with courage, bird sense and a great deal of style. Despite their being a little nearer the ground than the pointers and setters, and most of the other HPR breeds, they are quite capable of working the open hill for grouse as well as bashing through cover in search of rabbit or pheasant. The dense, slightly wavy coat serves them well as protection against the cold and against thorns and brambles, and dries quickly after a swim. It is claimed that they are less prone to ear troubles than some of our native spaniels, and their relatively sparse feathering should not collect too much in the way of mud, twigs, sweethearts and the like. As for their temperaments, well, let us say that they are sometimes temperamental.

The Brittany does not seem to have the same attachment to, and dependence on, human company as does the Vizsla or the Weimaraner. This can be quite disconcerting to the trainer when a Brittany pup shows little interest in the business of education, and even less inclination to co-operate. If you are used to the 'faithful hound' type reaction of a Labrador, then this casual indifference can be quite disconcerting. Once again, I must stress that these remarks are generalisations, and you may well find that your young Brittany is all attention and eagerness to please from day one. And then again, you may not.

They love to hunt, whether they are tracking down a runner or seeking fresh game with their heads high in the air, and this desire to hunt may be the reason that some are difficult to interest in the retrieving phase of their work. If you have one of these then you have several options: you can try the American training method of forced retrieving, you can carry on regardless with dummy exercises and hope that the penny drops eventually, or you can get on with the other aspects of training and trust that an interest in retrieving will manifest later. Everything depends on the temperament of the particular pup that you are training, and of course, your own temperament and attitude towards dog training.

A Brittany can be an annoying little brute at times, and a frustrating dog to train for any number of reasons, but with their energy and enthusiasm they are a joy to watch at work, when they are going well. With the pointing breeds, perhaps more than with any others, a great deal of the pleasure to be gained from a day's shooting is simply in watching the dog work, and on that basis alone the Brittany is worthy of consideration. If you are more interested in the retrieving than the game-finding side of dog work then a Brittany is probably not your best bet.

The Large Munsterlander

The Large Munsterlander is another of the more recent introductions to Britain, the breed first becoming established here in about 1971. They are big, strong dogs with a black and white coat similar to that found on a working English Setter, and it is a common mistake to assume that they are descended directly from setter ancestors. There may indeed be some setter blood in their background, breeding lines being so confused and poorly documented in the last century that it is very difficult to trace the origins of almost any gundog breed with complete confidence, but the primary source of the Munster is well known.

As well as German Shorthaired Pointers and German Wirehaired Pointers, there is a breed known as the German Longhaired Pointer, which for some reason has not yet found favour with those who import new breeds to this country. The German Longhaired Pointer is only permitted to have a liver and white coat, though until the latter half of the nineteenth century the breed came in both liver and white and black and white. With the fashion for setting standards prevalent at the time the breeders of GLPs decided that only liver and white was acceptable, a decision that left the black and white dogs somewhat out in the cold. Other breeders, unwilling to condemn a dog simply because of the colour of its coat, took an interest in the black and white cast-offs, and the Large Munsterlander was christened, taking its name from an ancient province of Germany which bordered Holland. The 'Large' part of the name was added to distinguish the dogs from a similar, but smaller, breed which was also being developed, and which is known as the Small Munsterlander.

The Large Munsterlander is always black and white, and the German Longhaired Pointer is always liver and white. Straightforward and simple? Yes, excepting that they have common ancestors and the fact that German Longhaired Pointer blood is still sometimes introduced into Munster lines. The not surprising result of this is that Large Munsterlander litters will sometimes contain the odd liver and white puppy which, at least in theory, is a German Longhaired Pointer. And there are sometimes even tricoloured dogs, which are technically neither one nor the other. All of which is really irrelevant as far as the suitability of the breed for shooting is concerned.

The Munster, like the GSP, the GWP and the Weimaraner, is a dog which has been developed to suit the type of shooting which is popular with the sportsmen of Germany. Their shooting day might embrace both snipe and red stag, and quite a lot in between, and they require dogs which are versatile enough to both find, point and retrieve the snipe, and then to track down the stag if it should happen to be wounded or shot among thick woodland. They have bred their dogs accordingly, and have rigorously applied standards through which they try to ensure that their working breeds are kept as useful and versatile working dogs.

A Large Munsterlander is, as the name suggests, a big dog, long on the leg, strong, and capable of covering a lot of ground, with the stamina needed for long days in the field. Their thick coats give them an obvious advantage over HPRs such as the Weimaraner or GSP when they are asked to face thick cover, or to retrieve from icy water, though it might be less of an asset in the course of a long, hot day at the grouse in August. They are intelligent and sensitive dogs, and have the reputation for being picky feeders, though they are certainly not alone in this respect.

The Italian Spinone

Another recent and very distinctive addition to the list of Hunt, Point Retrievers available in Britain is the Italian Spinone. The Spinone has a very thick and wiry coat, quite a bit longer than that of a German Wirehaired Pointer with which they share the prominent moustaches, beards and eyebrows which give both breeds an extremely attractive expression. Big dogs – they weigh up to around eighty pounds – they are usually white, or some combination of white and orange, brown or roan.

It is not only their appearance which is different from the other, more familiar HPR breeds, but also their way of working. Spinones are not expected to produce the racing gallop of a GSP or a Brittany at work, but rather to proceed at a fast trot with only the occasional burst of enthusiasm to lift them into a gallop. It is a rather peculiar gait, but one that it would be easy to get used to, particularly if the dog in question was finding plenty of birds.

Opinions differ as to their origins, one theory being that they are direct descendants of setters which have developed the long coat as protection against the cold. In Italy? More likely perhaps, they are also said to have descended from the Coarsehaired Segugio, from the Griffon, or from Coarsehaired Setters introduced from the Adriatic by traders, and then crossed with a white mastiff. Their coats make them impervious to cold and wet, and they are said to be particularly good at working in swampland, or where dogs are required to retrieve from thick cover. Their stamina is rated exceptionally highly, and this, combined with their relatively slow pace, should see a Spinone covering a lot of ground in the course of a day's work, more in the end perhaps than many faster dogs which run out of steam after a few minutes, or a few hours.

They sound like an attractive proposition for the sportsman who likes to take his day at an easy pace and perhaps enjoys snipe shooting on an Irish bog or among the fens and washes of East Anglia. In field trials they will need assessing by judges who appreciate the style and standard of work expected from a Spinone, rather than that which is required from a GSP or a Vizsla. Not, you understand, that I am suggesting the Spinones will have to be judged against a lower standard, simply against a different one.

Hunt, Point and Retrieving Work

I have referred earlier to the American designation for HPR breeds as Versatile Hunting Dogs, and I make no apology for mentioning it again. The HPR breeds, and particularly those with German origins such as the GSP, GWP, Large Munsterlander and Weimaraner, are the result of a lot of dedicated breeding aimed at producing a single dog that can carry out a wide range of tasks, and carry them all out effectively. This versatility was not an original requirement of all HPR breeds, and some are naturally less versatile and more specialised than others. For competition purposes, though, we lump them altogether under the blanket designation of Hunt, Point Retrievers.

This is a little like running trials for 'Dogs Which Hunt and Retrieve' and asking spaniels and retrievers to compete together. Would you then eliminate a Labrador if it failed to face cover with the same alacrity as a Springer, or dump a Cocker Spaniel if it found retrieving a hare a less simple task than did a Flatcoat? Obviously there would have to be compromise, just as there has to be in HPR trials where the quartering of a Spinone has to be judged alongside that of a Brittany or a GSP.

For the practical shooting man one of the HPR breeds might seem to be a natural choice, combining the work of the spaniels and the retrievers with that of the pointing dogs, a dog which can roust out rabbits and pheasants on a rough shoot or beaver away in the beating line for driven pheasants, sit by your side in a hide or at a peg until asked to retrieve, or quarter a hill in search of grouse. Any of the Hunt, Point Retrievers described above should be capable of doing all those things, given the proper training, the necessary work experience, and given that you get a dog which has the latent ability in the first place.

The different HPR breeds all have their strengths and weaknesses, and it is up to the individual gun to decide which of the breeds is the most likely to be suited to his particular mixture of types of shooting. If most of your sport takes place on a grouse moor then I would suggest that a Spinone or a Weimaraner is unlikely to be the first choice, just as the thinner coated breeds such as GSPs are not suited to wildfowling. More important, though, is the question of whether one of these versatile breeds is the right choice for you in the first place.

The retrieving breeds, the spaniels and the pointers and setters, have all been bred to be specialists in their particular types of gundog work. Their size and shape are designed to maximise their efficiency at their work, their temperaments to suit them for the type of work they have to perform. They have thick coats to protect them against cold and cover, thin coats to allow them to work under a hot August sun or dense, oily coats to guard them from freezing seawater. Their scenting powers are suited to their work, be it pointing grouse fifty yards away on air scent or tracking a wounded pheasant on foot scent an hour or so after it passed by. As the ability to perform one task is refined and enhanced, so the ability to perform another may be diminished, but it is of no matter. They are specialists, and their function is to specialise.

But the HPR breeds are required to be all things to all men, to have long scenting noses for pointing work, yet be able to get the head down to track game on its foot scent. They are asked to work in the heat of the summer or the cold of a winter's day, to sit quietly as non-slip retrievers or to bash through thorns and brambles like a spaniel. They need the courage to face a wounded stag or a boar yet the soft mouths to retrieve game without damaging it. They need the strength to force their way through thickets yet the lightness and balance to quarter the hill without damaging joints and tendons. They must know that a grouse or a partridge in the open must be pointed, but that a pheasant in thick cover may have to be flushed without benefit of an initial point, that today they have to quarter the open stubbles while tomorrow their job is to root along the hedge bottom. They have to be built in such a way that they are physically capable of doing all these things, and have the temperament to switch from an active to a passive role when required. It takes a very special dog to be capable of doing all those things. It also takes something a little extra in the trainer and handler to get the best, or anything close to the best, out of such a dog.

You can, of course, select one of the HPR breeds solely as a beating dog, or a picking-up dog, or a rough shooting dog, or a grouse dog, a retriever or tracker for wounded deer. If you get the right dog, and have the ability to train it, then there is every chance that you will get a dog which can do the job you want. But, and it is an important but, the chances are that you would have ended up with a better dog if you had chosen one of the specialists in the first place. Your dog may be quite happy performing its limited role, but it is probably only being used to a quarter of its potential.

I see little sense in choosing a pointing dog and then using him solely to flush game within gunshot like a spaniel, but I have met a number of HPR owners who insist that this is the proper role of their dogs. It is not. I was once informed, by someone who should certainly have known better, that a Vizsla was like a Brittany, and should never hunt more than thirty yards from its handler. Such an attitude is nonsense, and a nonsense made worse by the fact that the person in question was a very prolific producer of Vizsla puppies. Little wonder that some Vizslas have the reputation of being poor quarterers. If, though, you have the variety of shooting, and perhaps stalking, that can allow one of these versatile breeds to do its work to the full, then one of the HPRs is the natural choice.

Most HPR owners are owner/trainers – they train and work the dogs themselves. Many of the HPR breeds do tend towards being 'one-man dogs', and as such are not particularly suited to being sent away for professional training, nor for training up and selling as finished dogs. There are professional trainers who will accept an HPR into their establishments, but if you do decide to have your pup tutored in this way it is important to ensure that your chosen trainer understands the difference between Pointer Retriever work and that done by the more usual run of working gundog.

Another reason why so many HPRs are owner trained is the sheer length of time needed to take a raw novice to something approaching a finished dog. The curriculum is necessarily longer, and some parts, such as the natural instinct to point, have firstly to be inherited and then 'discovered' by the dog itself. You do not teach a pointing dog to point, you only encourage him to do what comes naturally. Many trainers do not have the time or the ground to give a novice HPR the necessary experience to turn it into a finished dog, and while the owner trainer can (and often does) spend years in bringing on a young dog the average professional trainer has to turn out the finished product in a somewhat shorter timescale.

That said, there are professional trainers who can, and do, take on an HPR and produce a good, workmanlike dog at the end of the training period. However, most HPR owners do their own training, and many do it to a very high standard indeed. Bear in mind though, particularly if you are new to training gundogs, that training a Pointer Retriever to work at anywhere near its potential is a far more demanding business than training the average Labrador to be a non-slip retriever. If you get it right, eventually, it is a whole lot more satisfying too.

Training

In order that we don't start out at cross purposes let me say, right at the beginning, that this is not a chapter which sets out to tell you how to train a dog. There are any number of books – whole books – which will do that for you: *Training Spaniels, Training Retrievers, Training Labrador Retrievers, Training the Pointer Retriever, Training Pointers and Setters, Training Pointers and Setters for Field Trials, Gundog Training for Beginners, Advanced Gundog Training, Gundog Problems Solved*; the list is long, comprehensive, and getting longer every year. The shooting man who seeks advice on gundog training need look no further than his local library or bookshop.

In addition to the many contemporary books there are also plenty of older volumes which deal with the subject. The work that is required of a spaniel, retriever, pointer or setter has changed little over the past century or so: a good dog by the standards of 1895 would still be a good dog by the standards of 1995. It might well be a better dog than most of the current crop, though there is no way to decide that particular question. The attitude of the shooting man towards his dog may have changed in the intervening years, as has our attitude to shooting itself, but the end product – a well trained dog – is much the same now as it was then, and the problems that have the modern trainer tearing his hair will be the same ones that induced premature baldness in his predecessors.

True, the terminology has changed. One of the classic manuals on dog training is Major-General W. N. Hutchinson's *Dog Breaking*, published by John Murray in 1848. Imagine the outcry that would arise if a modern author used such a title with all its implications of cruelty and harsh treatment for man's best friend. Of course, things were different in those days. Or were they?

The Victorian era certainly had its fair share, probably more than its fair share, of cruel and thoughtless dog trainers who used fear and punishment to cow their charges into obedience. Dog whips were freely advertised along with leads and collars and kennels and dog food and all the other paraphernalia that goes with dog keeping. Many owners had a much less sentimental view of their working dogs than is usual today, buying and selling dogs as a matter of course, and putting them down as soon as their working life was over. The dog, for some, was just a tool to be used and discarded when done with. Yes, by modern standards some of the Victorians were undoubtedly cruel, but they were not typical of all, or even of the majority, of gundog owners. There were plenty of owners and trainers around then, as there are now, who treated their dogs with kindness, and produced well trained and capable working dogs without constant resource to the whip or the stick. And there are still trainers around today who use the worst of the Victorian methods to bring their pupils on. You may not be able to order a dog whip through the post anymore, but you can cause just as much distress with the end of a lead or a stick from the hedgerow as you can with a purpose-built whip. And let us not forget that somewhat controversial product of modern technology, the electronic training collar. I wonder what the Victorian dog breakers would have thought of it?

The most important thing to understand about training a dog is that there are two individual personalities involved in the process – your own and that of the dog. There can be no simple, blanket set of instructions which will enable you to train a dog. There are plenty of good books that will tell you what you want to achieve, and even how you may achieve it with different types of dog, but there is no book so specific that it can analyse your individual temperament, cross-reference it to the temperament of the particular puppy that you are attempting to train, and provide you with detailed instructions to follow. If you are going to train a dog, then you have to analyse that particular dog's personality and decide how to proceed, bearing in mind of course your own temperament, ability and experience at training dogs.

Be wary of books that set out a timetable for training a puppy. I am thinking of a particular book that had the whole of the training cycle, from the first basic steps to the introduction to the shooting field, all laid out in detail, week by week and month by month. At 'x' months of age you began basic obedience work; at 'y' months you started dummy retrieves; after 'z' weeks of running the pup on a line you were ready to introduce it to live game. The whole process was there, right up to the day that you had the first bird shot over your newly qualified pupil. Now, as far as the actual instructions for training went, the book was neither better nor worse than many another. The problem was in the assumption that your puppy would progress at exactly the same rate as the author's hypothetical puppy, be quite reliable on the drop whistle at the same time, be ready to take to the shooting field proper at the same age. The assumption was that the reader would take just the same length of time to get each lesson across to his puppy as the author had to his own. If not, then the reader was going to be rushing on to the next lesson before the current one was fully absorbed, and there is no surer way to ruin a gundog than to rush through the training process before the dog is ready. So let us not rush our fences. Before setting out on a journey it is generally a good idea to have some notion of the final destination. If you are training a puppy it makes sense to start by thinking about what you want as the end result.

Now the obvious reply might seem to be 'a trained gundog'. Agreed, but what do you mean by 'trained'? Should the dog sit, instantly and unquestionably, at the slightest peep of the drop whistle, the merest suggestion of an upraised hand, or will it be good enough if it will sit after three long blasts on the Thunderer and a couple of throat-rasping shouts? Do you care whether it will sit to order at all as long as it can find game and flush it? Is it essential to you that you can handle the dog out on to a precise spot two hundred yards away, then send it left or right with whistle or hand signal? Or do you leave all that fancy stuff to the pickers-up and just concentrate on the dead birds around your peg? Must your dog drop instantly to wing or to shot, or will you be quite content as long as it doesn't actually get into the line of fire when it runs in? Does walking to heel mean walking with the nose a precise six inches behind your left heel, or does it mean the dog is somewhere in sight and not actually chasing anything? Does every retrieve require a perfect, sitting delivery, or are you happy if the bird gets spat out somewhere where you can find it again without too much trouble. And do you expect to be able to send the dog for multiple retrieves in the order that you want them collected, or do you leave that sort of executive decision to the dog himself?

The way in which you train your dog, and the time it is going to take, will obviously depend on which of those extremes you favour. Indeed, there are plenty of owners whose dog training programme is simply to take the dog and the gun out on the first day of the season, turn the dog loose and commence training from there. And it has to be said, those owners are quite often perfectly happy with their dog's standard of work. Of course, their shooting companions may have a slightly different viewpoint.

You can shoot over a totally untrained dog. It will probably flush game for you, perhaps point it first if it is one of the pointing breeds. The same untrained dog may well retrieve what you shoot. If you are lucky with your choice of pup, and there is sufficient natural ability there to start with, you may even end up with a better dog than the one on which your neighbour has just lavished two years of patient instruction. You may do, but the chances are that you will not. The chances are that you will end up with something that ruins the day for you, for your shooting companions, and for all the well trained dogs that have to sit and grind their teeth while your little treasure races about, flushes game out of shot, steals other dog's retrieves, and generally makes sure that you won't be invited back next year. Unless, of course, you happen to be the host.

You may wonder why anyone would choose to take the trouble to acquire a puppy, to rear it, feed it and exercise it daily yet not take the trouble to teach it even the rudiments of discipline. Training a dog may be a lengthy process in that it takes several months, even years, to complete, but it need take no longer than a few minutes each day throughout those months or years. And for most of the time no special facilities are needed. All it takes is you, the pup and a few minutes of your time. Even so, there are, and there will always be, some owners who don't believe in 'suppressing a dog's natural ability' by wasting time in training it. Having had first-hand experience of one or two dogs with an excess of 'natural ability' I prefer the dog which has had the benefit of that few minutes each day. Especially if I have to shoot with it.

At the opposite end of the dog training spectrum lies the field trial enthusiast. To win at trials, particularly at retriever trials, requires a dog which can demonstrate a very high standard of response and obedience to its handler. It requires a great deal more as well, including natural ability and sometimes a certain amount of luck, but for the moment we are concerned with the training aspect. Whether the stake is for retrievers, spaniels, HPRs or pointers and setters, one of the requirements needed to satisfy the judges is to show that the dog is under the control of the handler, and not vice versa. The control may be a little tenuous at an HPR or pointer and setter stake, but the principle remains. If you cannot control your dog then you will not win field trials. Or not very often.

It is not unknown for those who train and work gundogs without getting involved in the field trials scene to dismiss trialling dogs as overtrained and lacking in the initiative and self-reliance needed by a 'proper' shooting dog, and there is some justification for their argument. I once saw a pheasant dropped ten yards inside a woodland edge. It was flapping in its death throes and could be heard quite clearly. The handler was asked by the judge to send his dog for the retrieve. The dog was all eagerness, ears pricked at the sound of the bird flapping and just waiting for the instruction to cross the few yards between it and the bird. The handler hesitated, then said 'Can you give me a line on it please?' The judge, to his credit, grunted once, then replied, 'Just send the bloody dog.' The 'bloody dog' did what was required of it with no further assistance. Yes, it is a very useful skill to be able to handle your dog to exactly where you want it, but it is a skill that should be tempered with moderation. There is no need to guide a dog to the fall when it has already marked the bird, and there is a danger that too much handling can eventually destroy a dog's initiative, or prevent the dog from ever developing the ability to think for itself. But, and it is a very important but, there are times when you may really need to handle your dog out to an unmarked bird, across a river perhaps, and when the ability to do so can make the difference between a lost bird and a bird in the gamebag.

Suddenly those 'showy' field trial tricks won't seem quite so showy any more.

Overhandling is a common fault among some trialling competitors. Perhaps even more common is the handler who punctuates the whole of their dog's run with a constant stream of whistle commands, most of which are ignored. Attempted overhandling impresses no one, least of all the dog, yet the sound of a turn whistle in constant employment is a familiar one at many trials. There may be a good reason: the judge may have asked you to work a restricted beat which means that the dog has to be turned short of its natural pattern, but a more likely cause is a nervous handler. Out shooting it is much to be preferred if the dog can be left to hunt on its own initiative, without constant peeping from a whistle, provided of course that its initiative guides it into performing a reasonable standard of ground coverage. But suppose you have to work a piece of ground bordering a busy road? It might be useful if you could blow your turn whistle then and be confident that your dog would answer before it started playing dodgems with the traffic.

Some of the requirements of the field trial dog may seem a little over the top when applied to the average shooting man's dog. Perfect steadiness, instant obedience, total rapport with the handler at all times; they sound great in theory, but do we really need such refinements for a day roughing around the hedgerows? If the dog isn't steady to fall of game we can always tether him while we are at our peg. If he won't stay at heel we can always put a lead round his neck. If he won't come when he's called we can always . . . keep calling? Not let him off the lead? Let him go anyway and hope that he won't ruin the next drive? Perhaps there is something to be said for the well trained dog after all. You never know, you might even decide to have a go at a field trial with him.

Assuming that you are not one of those brave souls who relies entirely on 'natural ability' in lieu of proper training, we might turn our attention to training itself, the 'how' and the 'when' instead of the 'if' and the 'why'. There is, as I have already said, lots of advice available, whether you are a novice or an expert. Books have been around for centuries, there is a recent surge of videotaped instruction packages on the market, and there is that old favourite the dog training class, which should really be called the dog's owner training class. In addition some of the gundog breed societies run training forums for their members, and some professional dog trainers offer private instruction. Alternatively, you might just prefer to get on with it by yourself and learn as you go along.

The first thing to do is to get clear in your own mind exactly what it is you want the dog to do once the training is finished. And yes, I know that training is never truly finished, so let us say what stage do you want the dog to reach before you are ready to consider it as a working gundog rather than as a gundog in training? Some of the decisions that you make now may have an important bearing on how you conduct your training. Perhaps you want a non-slip retriever, solely for picking up at driven shoots. You don't want to mess about with leads and tethers every time you change pegs, so you will concentrate very hard on steadiness; steadiness on the drop and steadiness at heel. 'Heel' must mean just that: nose against your left heel and kept there, whatever the temptation, and 'Stay' means stay right there for the rest of the day if necessary. No problem there. But suppose you are training one of the HPR breeds, a pointer or a setter. Too much heelwork, too much steadiness training might just produce a dog which will be reluctant to get out and quarter the ground a hundred, two hundred, three hundred yards away from you. Natural ability can sometimes be stifled with an overabundance of obedience work.

You must also assess your pupil. There is, as we have seen, an awful lot of advice and instruction available to you. The trouble is, all too often there is conflicting advice and instruction. Take the matter of getting your dog to hunt. Some books will tell you that the pup should never encounter live game until it is perfectly steady and totally reliable on the drop whistle. Sound, rational advice, with clear logic behind it. If the dog is never allowed to chase game he will never form the habit of chasing. Get him one hundred per cent obedient to the drop whistle and then let him see his first rabbits or pheasants. When they run or fly you blow the drop whistle, and soon enough, by association, the pup will be dropping to wing like a veteran. And so he very well may, provided that he really was one hundred per cent reliable on that drop whistle. Of course, you won't know that he is reliable in the face of temptation until you've tried – in the face of temptation – but the method is sound, and it does work.

Except that some other books will tell you that it is more important to allow the pup to develop his natural hunting instincts first, before you start to try and mould the obedience side of his training. So now you let the dog out to hunt freely until you are sure that the desire to hunt is properly established, then you start the steadiness work. The logic is that the pup isn't learning to disobey when he is free hunting because you are not trying to stop him. That aspect comes later. Again, the method works in some cases. In other cases . . . well, let us just say that it may not be the simplest of tasks to curb that enthusiasm for hunting and chasing when the time comes to instil the necessary manners. The truth is that there are some dogs which would benefit from the first method and others which might be better trained with the second. A bold extrovert might well need keeping under tight control unless he is to take control altogether, while a shyer, more nervous dog might need the stimulus of free hunting if it is ever to build the confidence to get out and work on its own initiative. What you must do is to assess the character of your particular dog, and decide which (if either) of the two regimes is likely to suit it.

You must also decide when to start training. Some books will tell you six months, some sooner and some later. They are all correct, for some dogs, and they are all wrong for others. You start training when the dog is ready to absorb the lessons. This may be at six months for some dogs and at a year and a half for others, and no book can tell you which is the right age for your puppy. You have to decide.

Training a gundog is not a complicated process, unless you decide to make it complicated. I saw someone quite recently out walking a Labrador and trying, with a conspicuous lack of success, to get the dog to sit to a whistle command. Owner and dog were both novices, and had been attending their local dog training classes. They had been instructed that there should be one command to be used to get the dog to sit when it was away from them and another to get it to sit when it was walking at heel, plus a drop command to be used at a distance and a drop command for use during heelwork. Oh yes, and there were four separate voice commands as well as the four whistle commands. And they were trying to teach them all at the same time instead of getting one properly established before going on to the next. Needless to say, it wasn't working. Now it is quite likely that, had they taken their time, they might well have got the dog to learn, and respond to, all eight different commands. The question is, why would they want to? If you want your dog to sit, then the same command will serve whether the dog is half a yard or half a mile away. Certainly the dog needs to respond to either your voice or your whistle, but I can see no possible justification for having separate commands for when the dog is near and when it is further off. Unfortunately my friends, and all the other pupils at their dog training classes, were being taught this by the 'expert' who ran them.

It is important to distinguish between those things that have to be taught when training a dog, and those which the dog has to learn for itself. The sight of a pointer suddenly hitting the scent of grouse and slamming on to point, stopping instantly from a full gallop, is always impressive, and never more so than when seen for the first time. I couldn't guess at the number of times I have been asked, 'How do you teach them to point?' The answer is always the same: 'You don't.' Pointing dogs point naturally, or they don't point at all. You can encourage them to hold steady when they have pointed, you can lead them up to where you know there is game to try and induce them to point, but in the end, if they won't point then they won't point. But they nearly always will, several hundred years of selective breeding having been devoted to just that end.

But back to the training programme. As I have already suggested, it makes a lot of sense to get clear in your own mind exactly what you want from the dog, and tailor your training programme accordingly. Obviously, if your eventual aim is to win honours in field trials you will need a considerably more extensive training programme than if you want a dog solely for use in the beating line. A Pointer Retriever which is to be used to its full capabilities is going to take a lot more training than a dog which will only be required for retrieving duties. You know what you want from your dog, so you must set the agenda.

Certain basic training exercises will almost certainly be necessary, whatever your final intentions are for the dog. Every gundog should be trained to sit, or drop, on command, to return to its handler when called, and to stay when ordered. Note that all three things must be taught to the dog; they do not come naturally. Pointing, retrieving, quartering, finding game or tracking it are natural abilities that have to be harnessed to our use, but they are all things that a working gundog will do naturally. The distinction is important. Let me quote a passage from a favourite book of mine which says it much better than I can. The author is Robert Ruark, the book is *The Old Man and The Boy*, and the subject is training a pointer which the 'Old Man' had just bought for his grandson.

'"A bird-dog," the Old Man told me, "is trained in the back yard. There ain't no way in the world you can teach him to smell; so you don't have to bother about that. There ain't no way in the world you can teach him bird sense; so there ain't any use worrying about that. All you can teach this dog is a little discipline, so that he can use his talents to the best advantage."'

'A little discipline' is the most important thing in training any gundog, not just the bird-dogs but all gundogs. If your pup will sit when told, stay where he is told and come to you when you call, and will do those three things whatever the temptation to do something else more interesting and exciting, then he is well along the road to being a trained dog. No, I don't mean there is nothing else for him to learn, but if those three commands are clearly understood and obeyed then they will be a considerable help in getting over the later, more interesting lessons like quartering and retrieving.

The discipline is mainly taught by repetition: you give the 'sit' command with your pup safely attached to you by a lead, then you push his backside down until he is sitting. A little praise, then you give the 'heel' command and you walk a little further, then you do it again. And again, but not so often that the dog loses interest and starts to disobey out of sheer boredom. A few minutes of this, once or twice a day, is ample. Five minutes twice a day for six days is infinitely better than six days of nothing followed by sixty minutes of concentrated work on the seventh.

You don't have to be actually 'training' in order to train the dog. You can use that 'sit' command before you give him his food bowl, before you let him through a door, or into the car, or before you take the lead off to let him have a run round the park. Gradually it should become almost automatic; then you introduce the whistle, the one you are going to use to stop the dog. Some people like a single, long blast on their turn whistle to act as a sit/down command. There is logic in this. You only need to carry one whistle, which avoids confusion when the dog is setting out in hot pursuit of something small and furry. On the other hand, there are those folk who prefer a good, loud blast from an Acme Thunderer, reasoning that there is no excuse for the dog failing to hear that, nor any doubt about what command is being given. Except that some shoots use three blasts on a Thunderer to signal the end of a drive, and you may be unpopular if you call a halt to proceedings when all you wanted to do was get your dog to sit for a moment.

You do the same sort of thing for the 'stay' command, sitting or dropping your dog and then moving away, about a yard, while keeping eye contact and saying 'stay', or 'wait', or 'steady', or whatever command you want to use. If he gets up you put him back again; if he stays you go back to him and praise him. Note particularly that you go back to the dog; you don't call the dog to you at this stage. If you do, and you praise him for coming when called, then he is liable to start anticipating the command and coming before he is called. Then what? Praise him for coming to you and make the habit worse, or tell him off and give him the idea that he doesn't want to come to you because he will get a rollicking? If he does break from the stay just take him firmly in hand and put him back where he was, repeat the command to stay and don't go quite so far away this time.

But there are any amount of books which will give you full chapter and verse on the mechanics of training a pup. The first thing is to instil some manners – that little bit of discipline we were talking about earlier – and the way to instil discipline is by repetition. Simple commands, regular lessons, and not going on to the next lesson until the current one is properly understood and absorbed. And even when a lesson has been learned the discipline still has to be reinforced on a regular basis, the basic commands used and the dog made to obey them. However good your eleven-month-old puppy may be at the basic lessons, unless you keep using, and enforcing, those basic commands even while you are moving on to the more advanced, more interesting stuff, it's a fair bet that they will have been forgotten after a month or three. Perhaps not 'forgotten', in that the pup will still know what the commands require of him, but he will have learned that he can ignore them if it suits him. And he will.

But you won't be letting him forget, will you? In any case, you will be using those basic commands as you progress to retrieving and hunting. Take the retrieve as an example. You 'sit' your pup and you tell him to 'stay' while you throw the dummy. Then you send him to fetch it, and you use your recall command to get him to bring it back to you, then the sit command again when he arrives. You might need to add something like 'hold it' if the pup has a tendency to spit the dummy out, or perhaps it will be 'give', or 'dead' if he prefers to hang on to it instead of handing it over. If the habit of coming to you when you whistle, or call, is firmly ingrained you can make use of this when encouraging your pup to quarter the ground properly, assuming that you are going to use him in a hunting role and will want him to quarter. First you encourage the pup to run off ahead of you, while the wind is on your cheek. Then you blow the recall whistle, turn through one hundred and eighty degrees and walk away from him. He should reach you; you encourage him to get on ahead again, then repeat the procedure. Quite soon you should have him quartering and turning on the whistle.

A word of warning: always be sure that you are encouraging the pup to quarter across the wind. Indeed, there is a very good chance that a working-bred pup will use the wind instinctively, and adapt his quartering as the wind shifts. What you do not want to do is to so brainwash your pupil that he will quarter at a right angle to your line of march irrespective of the wind direction. It might look pretty, but it's damned inefficient. Dogs find game by using scent, and scent is carried on the wind. Crossing the wind in a hunting pattern is the most effective way to find game, or residual traces of game.

Repetition is the basis of training, but it is possible to have too much repetition. Take retrieving lessons. There you are with dog and dummy; you sling the dummy out into the long grass and the dog goes and fetches it. Then you do it again, and again, and again, and eventually the pup decides that he's had enough of this particular game. So he either refuses to go and fetch, or else he adds a few little embellishments of his own, like taking the dummy for a couple of fast laps round the field and practising the old rat-killing shake with it. Either way you have a problem to solve, and it's a problem that you've created.

There are, as I said earlier, two sides to the education of a gundog. There are the things that you teach him, and there are the things that he has to learn for himself. Robert Ruark had it exactly right when he said that there was no point in worrying about the things that you can't teach. What you have to do is to work on the discipline until you feel that your pup is ready to get a look at the real thing. Now, depending on what you are going to use the dog for, the real thing may mean retrieving a bird or a rabbit that has just been shot, instead of picking up cold game that was killed the day before and hidden in the bushes especially for the dog to find, or it may mean being sent to quarter a covert, or a hillside, where there should be grouse, rabbit or pheasant to find and point, or flush. This is the point at which learning by repetition ends and learning by experience begins.

More dogs are ruined in the first day or two, or even hour or two, in the shooting field than by any other means. No matter how religiously you have followed the instructions in the book of your choice, no matter how good the pup is on his sits and stays, turns and recalls, the moment when he first encounters live game, serious gunfire and all the excitement of a shooting day is an incredibly severe test of discipline. If ever there was a moment when your full attention should be on your dog then this is it. And what are you doing? Searching the skies for the next pheasant to come rocketing out of the covert perhaps, while you hope the pup is sitting and staying like he did in training? Or maybe waiting with every muscle taut for the grouse to jump just ahead of the little pointer's nose, and trusting that he will drop to wing as well as he did when you were poised over him with the 'hup' command hovering on your lips?

Not if you've got any sense. There is no way that you can concentrate on your shooting and your newly trained but totally inexperienced dog. And there is no way that anyone should be waving a loaded gun about unless he is concentrating very hard on what is in line with the sharp end. So you give most of your attention to the pup, and shoot a beater? Hopefully not – I do a lot of beating, and it might be me. More likely you concentrate on the pheasants or the grouse, and the dog, seeing that he is effectively unsupervised, starts to improvise. He does whatever it seems natural for him to do. And all that discipline that you have been painstakingly attempting to instil is not natural. So your pup runs in, or charges off ahead and flushes birds, or pegs them, or takes himself off to chase a hare. And he enjoys it, and he associates that enjoyment with a shooting day. So what is he going to be looking forward to next time you go shooting? Hopefully you will also have enjoyed your day shooting, because the cost of that day may well have been the ruination of one gundog. For the next ten years or so you will be trying to cure the faults that were caused by that first day out in the shooting field.

There is an alternative scenario. Suppose that for the first few days when your pup was being introduced to his life's work you had left the gun in the cabinet and just taken the dog along? Then you could have concentrated one hundred per cent on your dog, and on ensuring that all those lessons which you spent so long on together would not be forgotten in the excitement of battle. And for the next ten years you might be able to concentrate on your shooting in the knowledge that the dog would be concentrating on his own job, and doing it properly.

However important those first few days in the shooting field may be – and there is no question of understating their importance – at the end of those first days you may have an obedient dog, but you will not yet have an experienced dog. You may have done your bit and trained the dog to the limit of your abilities, but now the dog has to get on and learn all the tricks of his trade so that you can both discover the extent of those abilities.

You can't teach a dog to know when a bird has been pricked by shot but shown no obvious signs of injury, but there are thousands of retrievers around the country which have this 'magical' ability to sense when a bird has been wounded. You can't teach a pointing dog that sometimes he needs to hold back off his birds because the heather is wet and the grouse are liable to jump at the slightest excuse, but given the experience many pointing dogs will develop this ability unbidden. One day they close their birds and point solidly in the position from which the birds will eventually flush; another day and they stop on the slightest whiff of scent and wait, with their tail waving gently, until the guns come up. Then they rode forward, perhaps twenty yards, perhaps a hundred, until the birds rise, hopefully in shot. Or perhaps he can dive into the middle of twenty live pheasants and unerringly pick out the one which has been wing-tipped. The dog can learn to do it, but you and I can't teach him. There is no substitute for experience.

You may, however, want to consider the amount of experience that you are going to give your dog, especially in his first season. It is very tempting, once the first few days are successfully negotiated and the pup is showing promise, to use him at every opportunity. There is no substitute for experience, but it is quite possible to overdose on experience, particularly with a young dog. And, particularly if you are training one of the Hunt, Point and Retrieve breeds, there is also the question of which aspect of its work you begin to gain experience on.

This is one of those rather vexed questions which have several possible answers, any of which may be correct. There is one school of thought which maintains that you only allow the dog to hunt and point for its first season – two seasons? – because sending it for the retrieve is likely to encourage unsteadiness and running in to shot. Sound sensible and logical? Then what about the other alternative which has the dog doing nothing but retrieves, under strict control, for that first season or two, so that it is perfectly steady before you let it get out and start hunting. And that too is sensible and logical, since it is clearly easier to enforce discipline on a dog which is sitting by your heels than on one which is quartering a couple of hundred yards away from you. Then you have the well known axiom of the retriever trainer of never letting the dog go for anything other than a dead bird in its first season, the reason being to guard against the young dog getting a peck or a spur from a runner which could make it hardmouthed. It makes sense, except that I have seen an awful lot of 'stone dead in the air' birds that turned out to be very much alive and running as soon as they hit the ground.

I suppose it all comes down to using common sense, and your own judgement, which probably means putting a bit of a curb on your enthusiasm, at least for the first season. You are unlikely to do too little with an inexperienced dog, but it is all too easy to do too much. A friend, who is a very, very experienced trainer and handler of gundogs, was once asked to write a book on 'correcting faults in gundogs'. He turned down the commission, and I wondered why. The reason, he said, was simple. Once a fault is established the chances are that you will never correct it. The secret of good gundog training, therefore, is to ensure that the fault is never allowed to occur in the first place. That, though, may be easier said than done. Take hare chasing. Now the logical thing is not to give your dog the opportunity of chasing a hare until you are quite confident that the basic obedience is so ingrained that a blast on the stop whistle will end the chase. Fine; but what if you are out taking the pup for a bit of exercise and a hare leaps up all unbidden from right under his nose? However good your intentions it is always possible for something unforeseen to happen and scupper your plans.

The ideal may be to ensure that the pup is never in a position to make a mistake, but the reality is sure to be a little different. If training a dog was really just a matter of repetition and avoiding temptation then it might be a lot easier, but it would also be a lot less interesting. And the end result, when you and the pup do both get things right, would be a lot less satisfying. It is sometimes said that if a thing is too easy it is not worth doing in the first place. On that basis, training a gundog will always be very worthwhile.

Gundogs at Work

Gundog work, reduced to basics, is a very simple matter. A working gundog does one (or both) of two things. It finds live game so that it can be shot, and it recovers the dead or wounded game once it has been shot. The manner in which it performs the two tasks will depend on the breed of the dog; the skill with which it performs will be dependent on its natural ability, training and experience.

The work of the dog will vary according to the quarry that is being hunted and the terrain, and in Britain gundogs were developed especially to cope with particular combinations of the two. On the Continent, in direct contrast, dogs were developed to be able to work under a variety of conditions and to hunt a wide range of quarry. In theory, today's gundogs are still divided into specialists and all-rounders. In practice, some of the all-round breeds are asked to specialise, and the specialists to act as all-round gundogs.

Take the distinction between flushing dogs – the spaniels – and the retrieving breeds. The spaniels were developed as hunting dogs to search for live game and flush it; the retrievers were intended to collect the game after it was shot. Attend any driven shoot though and you are quite likely to find spaniels being used as retrievers and Labradors working in the beating line. I know one owner who had kept a team of Pointer Retrievers for many years and used them solely for picking up, and offhand I can think of four or five handlers who work German Shorthaired Pointers but won't allow them to retrieve. My own Labrador spends a lot more time in the beating line than she does working as a retriever, and in the past few years we have had a couple of Pointers which have seen service as beating dogs on driven pheasant shoots.

Before any purists throw up their hands in horror, let me say that I am well aware that a Pointer is not the right dog to push pheasants over a line of guns. Not only do you stand a fair chance of losing the dog when it points in the middle of a rhododendron thicket, but the spaniels in the beating line quickly learn what it means when the big, white dog stands still. If a spaniel or two nips in to flush the bird every time your dog points then you have a fairly certain recipe for inducing unsteadiness. However, we used the

Pointers because there was a real need for any dog that could find birds and get them into the air, and apart from a Labrador they were all that we had available at the time. As for unsteadiness, all of them were used after they had been retired from the hill, and at a time in their lives when it didn't matter if they were steady or not. I would never, under any circumstance, have taken a young pointer or setter out to work in the middle of a crop of sundry Labradors and spaniels, but as it happened the pointers did a good enough job. More important perhaps, they enjoyed their time in the beating line and got a few days back at work which they would not otherwise have had.

Sometimes there is no problem in using a dog to perform a task for which it is not ideally suited. Locally there are generally far more Labradors in the beating line than there are spaniels, though the spaniel is undoubtedly better suited to the task. The Labs may be a bit less efficient – perhaps leave a few birds behind that a team of Springers would have rousted out – but the majority of the birds get hunted out eventually, and if some are missed then there is always another day. Few owners have the space, or the inclination, to keep the 'right' dog for every different circumstance that may arise during their shooting season, and most dogs can be quite adaptable, given the chance. There are times, though, when the right dog is almost essential, or when the wrong way of working can be a positive detriment to a good dog.

Someone came to me a few years ago with a problem German Short-haired Pointer. The dog was apparently covering too much ground and getting too far ahead of the guns. I went across to see the dog working and was quite impressed: it got out well, found grouse, pointed them and held its points. True it was well ahead of us, but its ground treatment was more than adequate. So where was the problem? It seemed that she sometimes pointed well ahead of the line. The line? Yes, the dog was being worked ahead of a line of guns who were walking-up grouse. Did they ever walk-up birds that the dog had left behind? No, came the reply, they never did. And was she holding her points until they reached her? Oh yes; steady as a rock. So what was the problem? The guns didn't like to see the dog so far ahead in case she flushed birds. But she wasn't flushing birds, she was pointing them. So what was the problem?

The problem, in fact, was not with the dog, but because the shoot were confusing walking-up grouse with shooting grouse over pointing dogs. And to be fair, they were not alone in their mistake. Walking-up is one way to shoot grouse, dogging is another, and the two don't mix. Not only do they not mix, but it can be positively bad for a pointing dog to try and work it ahead of a line of guns. In some circumstances I have known it to be fatal – to the dog. A good friend saw one of her Irish Setters blinded when a careless gun shot at a bird which just happened to be in line with the dog which was working out ahead of the walking guns. There is only one future for a working dog with no sight.

Walking-up, whether your quarry is grouse, pheasant, snipe or hare, means walking, alone or in line, with a loaded gun and your dog – if you have a dog – hunting just ahead of the line and flushing anything that it finds. It means that you are walking across sometimes rough ground with a loaded weapon, and it requires exemplary attention to the safety rules. It can also be a bit of a soul-destroying pastime, particularly if you are walking-up on the type of grouse moor that has one pair of birds per thousand acres, but it is still a lot better than a day in the office. The main point though is that you have to be ready to shoot at any time since game may jump with little or no warning. Spaniels and retrievers working close to the line are fine for this type of shooting. Pointing dogs are most definitely not.

The whole reason for running a pointing dog is that it will find the game for you. Once it has found birds it will 'tell' you, by pointing, and then wait until you are ready to shoot before it flushes them. It will also, alone and unaided, cover at least the same amount of ground as eight or ten guns walking in line and working flushing dogs. Indeed, a good pointer or setter can be so efficient that at least one well known field sports writer has gone on record as suggesting that their use is unsporting. There is a good word for such an opinion; it is quite a short word, but I am not allowed to use it here. Back to dogging.

If you are shooting over a pointing dog, then the dog will, or should, find most, if not all, of the game on its beat, given half-decent scenting conditions and a half-decent dog. Since you do not have to assume the responsibility for finding and flushing game you and your fellow guns can wander along quite happily enjoying the scenery and the dog work, and keeping your guns empty until the dog comes on to point. Then, and only then, do you need to load your gun. It is a lot safer as well as being a lot easier and more congenial than walking in line. To begin with, there is no need to be constantly assessing your position in relation to the guns on either side. You can enjoy a conversation as you walk instead of marching along in lonely silence or risking disturbing the birds by hollering across to your neighbours. Nor do you spend half the day looking nervously down the muzzles of your neighbour's gun and hoping that the safety catch is on, and that he doesn't stumble.

Walking together will also help the dog to do its job better. It may not look that way, but when it is quartering the dog will have at least half an eye on its handler, and should structure its running pattern according to his position and line of march. Easy enough when the guns are all together, and the handler is walking a few yards ahead of them, but a lot more difficult when the guns are in a line spread across several hundred yards of the moor.

Being accustomed to hunting on either side of its handler, the dog may decide to extend its pattern to a couple of hundred yards beyond the last gun in line on either side. Then, unless the dog is moving very quickly, and the line walking very slowly, you will have to keep stopping and waiting for the dog to cross in front of you, or you will be walking through ground that has not yet been hunted. Alternatively, the dog will increase its forward cast to keep ahead of the line and miss birds because it is working beyond the limitations of its nose. When the dog does point, who goes to the point? The nearest two guns perhaps? What about the handler, who will almost certainly want to be there with his dog to make sure the guns are in the right position, then to click the dog on to hunt the birds out? It might take him a little while to reach the point, so you had better hope that the birds sit tightly, and the guns wait patiently until he arrives. If not, the dog may decide that this is a golden opportunity to have a little chase.

Shooting over bird-dogs is just about the most fun you can have standing up, but it is essentially a sport for a couple of guns only. If you have eight or ten guns all wanting to shoot grouse then walk in line by all means, but don't run a bird-dog ahead of the line. And please don't confuse walking-up with dogging, much less try to combine the two.

Working a pointer in the beating line at a pheasant shoot is a long way removed from bird-dog work, and although our old pointers are sometimes used as beating dogs they are far from ideal for the purpose. They are, though, better than no dog on the particular shoots where we work them; shoots which have only a few reared birds and a lot of woodland, and where the requirement is for a dog, any dog, that can find a pheasant and get it up in the air. Even I, with my fondness for pointing dogs in general, and Pointers in particular, must admit that a good spaniel would be far better at the job.

Beating can be a noisy, undisciplined walk through the woods, with dogs running every which way, or it can be a very carefully planned, quietly executed series of manoeuvres intended to flush the birds in a steady stream from a predetermined flushing point. It is not generally a good idea to introduce the tactics from the first type of beating on to a shoot where the keeper is looking for work of the second type.

At first sight work in the beating line might seem to be little more than taking the dog into a covert and turning it loose to hunt out the resident pheasants and flush them. In some coverts, on some shoots, that may be all that is required, and you could indeed take a practically untrained dog and let it do its own thing with the desired results. On other shoots, showing pheasants is almost an art form, and woe betide the dog that tears off ahead of the line out of control of the handler. Very often the first task of a beating line is not to flush pheasants at all, but to walk them along to the place from which they are to be flushed. Then, when there are a few dozen, or perhaps a few hundred pheasants all gathered in one place, the idea is to put them up a few at a time, not in one huge cloud that will sweep over the guns and be gone. The beaters will advance slowly and in line, tapping with their sticks and keeping their dogs close at heel until the birds are gathered at the flushing point. Then perhaps a single dog will be sent forward to push out the birds a few at a time with the rest of the beating team staying in position to prevent the birds running back. Sometimes, if the keeper judges that enough of his birds have been exposed to gunfire, for example, you may even be asked to let the dogs tear forward and flush the birds in a big cloud, but I would strongly advise that you make absolutely sure that that is what is wanted before you let your dog tear in.

This type of beating calls for very steady, well trained and well controlled dogs, though the job that they are doing is probably a lot easier than that asked of beaters' dogs on those shoots where birds are at a premium. Here the need may be simply to find the birds where they are skulking under brashing or in thick cover and to push them into the air. Now nose, experience and courage in facing cover are the skills required of the beating dog. A semi-comatose Labrador might be the ideal in the well-stocked coverts of a big shoot, but a bustling, hustling spaniel is probably nearer to the specification if there are only a couple of dozen wild and wily pheasants spread over forty acres of woodland.

An English Springer is probably the best dog for this type of work. Their constant optimism – the hope that, even if there hasn't been sight nor scent of a bird in the last twenty acres, there is sure to be one under the next bush, or the one after it – is just what is required. Pheasants can sit remarkably tightly at times, and it is all too easy for human beaters to pass all unknowing within a yard of a crouching bird. A good spaniel won't make the same mistake. The Cocker Spaniel can also be a grand little beating dog, though they tend to lack the optimism of the Springer and work better when there is some scent for them to work on.

Of course, beating dogs are by no means limited to Labradors, Springers and Cocker Spaniels, even if these are the most common. I know one handler who regularly works Irish Water Spaniels, and another who uses a Border Collie, while terriers of various kinds can be invaluable. Whatever your chosen breed though, it will be a better dog if it is kept under control than if it is allowed to run wild. Now that may seem to contradict what I was saying earlier about the type of shoot where dogs are vital to find a few birds and get them into the air. A mob of dogs running riot through the woods will certainly find birds and flush them, not to mention saving a few cartridges by making 'early retrieves', but they will not do their job nearly as efficiently as the same number of controlled and disciplined dogs working close to their handlers. For a start, a dog which tears about through the covert is not going to be hunting in any sort of systematic pattern, so birds are liable to be missed completely, particularly if they are tucked in tightly and prepared to let the beaters walk past them. Secondly, with the dogs running well ahead of the beating line birds may be chased back through the line instead of being sent in the proper direction. Thirdly, when birds are flushed they may be sent away from the guns instead of towards them, and fourthly, if your dog is working out of sight then you have handed over control of proceedings to the dog. There are times when you may have to do just that, but in general the right place for a beater's dog is working the ground just in front of the beater.

Pegging birds – grabbing them and 'retrieving' them instead of flushing them – is an all too common problem, particularly where the pheasants get trapped against a fence or are tucked tightly under thick cover which makes it hard for them to get their wings working initially. A dog which is used both for retrieving and for beating is asked at one moment to push birds into the air without touching them, and at the next to seize them and carry them back to the handler. It is not surprising if the dog sometimes muddles the two jobs, but it is far easier for the handler to guide the dog if it is working close by. Then you have a chance of anticipating the bird being pegged, and perhaps hupping the dog before the act. If the action is taking place a hundred yards ahead, your first intimation that a bird has been pegged will be when it is delivered to your hand.

Along with the delivery of the pegged bird comes a tricky little problem. Do you praise the dog for making the retrieve, or punish it for pegging the bird? Punishment is obviously out: your dog will associate the punishment with the last act it performed, i.e. delivering the bird to hand. All you are likely to achieve is to make the dog a reluctant retriever, or worse, a dog that pegs birds and then dumps them, dead or wounded, before the handler is aware that the bird has been lifted. In contrast, if the dog is working close in and under control, a firm 'no' at the moment when you think he is about to peg may have the desired effect of stopping him before the damage is done.

Control and discipline are just as important in a good beating dog as they are in any other working dog. If you can keep your dog under control and working the ground that you want it to work, then you will do a far better job together than if your dog tears off and does its own thing. While the dog is close to you, and under your control, he is not learning any bad habits from the other dogs, nor is he passing on any of his own. A beating line, particularly a beating line with a dozen dogs racing about completely at random, is a place filled with temptation for a young dog, and it is all too easy for a dog to be ruined by following the example of the other dogs in the line.

Birds flushed well ahead of a beating line still have a reasonable chance of flying in the right direction and giving the guns a shot. If you are using your spaniel for its original purpose and hunting out game for a walking gun, or pair of guns, then birds or rabbits flushed out of range are birds or rabbits lost, unless they are exceptionally sporting and elect to flush in the direction of your gun. A rough-shooting spaniel, or indeed any other dog, barring the pointing breeds, needs to work well within shotgun range. Taking the maximum range of a shotgun to be about fifty yards, this means that the rough-shooter's dog probably needs to stay within about thirty yards of him if he is to be given a reasonable chance of killing the quarry when it is flushed. Twenty yards might be a better bet in most cases.

Because a spaniel works close to its handler the need for proper ground treatment and use of the wind is less obvious than when shooting over one of the pointing breeds. When your dog is covering a couple of hundred yards to either side of you it is self-evident that the pattern of its quartering will determine how successful it will be in finding game. In contrast, a busy spaniel may look as if it is bound to find any game on its beat, irrespective of the pattern of its hunting. Nonetheless, the dog that uses the wind properly and hunts methodically should always be a more certain game-finder and a more efficient hunter than the one that mills about at random.

Here again, the difference between a Cocker and a Springer should be evident. A typical Springer may hunt every inch of ground, regardless of residual scent, or of how promising, or unpromising, the cover may look. By contrast, a Cocker is more likely to take a look around and assess the situation before starting out to hunt the most likely bits of cover. Cockers need scent to work on; Springers just need to believe that there might be some scent, somewhere. And again, I am generalising – there are plenty of Cockers that will work systematically and well, whether the cover is hooching with game or not, just as there are some Springers that need scent to get them going properly.

The primary requirement of a rough-shooting dog is the ability to find game and flush it, and to do this while close enough to the guns for it to be shot. If the dog doesn't do this part of his job then the next part, the retrieving phase, is likely to remain academic. When the shot is successful there is every chance that the retrieve will be a fairly simple one. The dog, having flushed the quarry, will undoubtedly be watching it closely, should have marked the fall automatically, and will probably be sent to pick the bird almost immediately. Even if it is a runner the dog is likely to be on the scent within moments of the wounded quarry setting off. Compare this with the work of the 'professional' retriever, the picking-up specialist.

Circumstances will obviously vary a great deal from shoot to shoot, and even from drive to drive, but the most likely place to find a picker-up is some way back behind the line of guns. The job of the picking-up dog is not usually to retrieve those birds which have been cleanly killed and dropped within a few yards of the gun, since many guns have their own dogs which they are anxious to use for these birds. It is the wounded birds, the runners, and those which sail off for half a mile into the distance before crumpling that are the lot of the picking-up dog.

A fresh scent from a runner may be a little known luxury for the picking-up dog, since it is common for the pickers-up to have to wait for the end of the drive before starting operations. Indeed, if the birds have dropped into a covert that is to be driven later, picking up may be left until the end of the day. Instead of going straight out to a marked retrieve the dogs may have to hunt 'blind' for any number of birds, and pick out the wounded from among dozens, perhaps hundreds, of undamaged birds which have dropped in to the same patch of cover.

The rough-shooting dog will usually be sent to retrieve almost as soon as a bird is shot. Quite a lot of rough-shooting dogs don't need to be sent for the retrieve since they will already be on the way by the time the first shot is fired. While not suggesting that running in is acceptable in any dog, it has to be admitted that there are degrees of acceptability. If you are out rough-shooting on your own, or with a friend, and your dog runs in to fall, then the odds are that little harm will result. If you are in a butt at a grouse moor, and your dog runs in after the bird you have just dropped behind the butt, there is a reasonable chance that it may get shot when you, or one of your neighbours, swings round to take a shot at the next covey to come low through the line. Grouse, with their low, contour-hugging flight, are particularly dangerous to the dog that runs in, or is sent for a retrieve before the drive has ended. Even on a pheasant drive though, it is far better if the retrieving dogs wait until they are sent before charging off to pick up and dead and the wounded. The dog that runs in rarely limits itself to those birds which fall within its limits of jurisdiction, and a lively discussion can soon get under way if two dogs run in after the same bird, and happen to arrive at the fall concurrently.

A good retriever needs to be a disciplined retriever. Yes, I know you can tether the dog down with a patent spike, or lash it to your belt, or your cartridge bag, but none of these measures can compare with the pleasure of having a well disciplined dog which sits patiently and waits for orders. Tying the dog to your belt is not really a good idea, particularly if the dog is liable to take a lunge just at the moment when you are lining the gun up on your right and left at woodcock, and the patent dog spike is a little difficult when you are a walking gun. Discipline is important in any gundog but, outside of field trials, it is probably the specialist retriever that is most improved by being properly behaved.

When there are a dozen or so birds to be picked at the end of a drive it is a great comfort if you can handle the dog out to the place where you want it to start hunting for a bird, or guide it on to the particular bird that you want picked first. If your dog simply charges about, out of sight, and turns up at intervals with a bird in its mouth, you will have little or no idea which of the downed birds has been picked. This may not seem like a problem until the Head Keeper comes up and wants to know if the hen that fell by the big oak tree in the corner has been gathered or not? A vague shrug of the shoulders will probably not be a sufficiently precise response.

There are times, at some shoots, where a well behaved retriever is effectively superfluous since every bird that falls is the prize in a race between a motley pack of loose dogs. This is extremely frustrating for the dog, sitting quietly and marking the birds, then seeing a neighbouring dog rush up and pick them, and can quickly result in the steady dog becoming unsteady. Frustrating too for the handler who, quite reasonably, likes to have his own dog retrieve the birds which he has shot. It requires an unusually equable temperament to remain silent when the carefully marked bird which was to be the young dog's first experience with freshly shot game is snatched up and borne away by some brute from three pegs down the line.

Such behaviour is bad for the dogs and bad for the shoot. The worst thing you can do is to turn your own dog loose to try and get some of 'his' retrieves before the others steal them, since it is a near certainty that he will end up joining in the general mêlée with the rest of the crew. At the end of the drive no one will know for sure which birds have been picked and which have been left. Even if the guns are accurate in their count of the numbers killed, and they will almost certainly not be, you will have no real idea where the missing birds are likely to be lying. Is it any wonder that the pickers-up give you an old-fashioned look when told that there are six, or possibly ten, birds to gather, somewhere, and some of them might be runners.

Picking-up can be one of the most enjoyable jobs on the shoot. Often you are back behind the line, away from all the other dogs and out of sight if something happens to go wrong. Provided that your dogs are well controlled, and that you know the programme well enough to be aware which coverts must not be disturbed, you can send them at once for the strong runners while marking the dead birds for collection at the end of the drive. Watching, really watching, what is happening will help you to do the job properly. Far better to be able to say to a gun that this is the cock bird that you touched with your second barrel, and this is the hen that fell by the hedge and ran into the wood, than simply to chuck another anonymous brace into the game cart.

Driven shooting can be a lot of fun for beaters and pickers-up as well as for the guns, but you and your dog will obviously have to fit in with the requirements of the keeper or shoot captain. Shooting in company means that your dog will be judged by someone else's standards; if you shoot alone then you have only yourself to satisfy. This does not necessarily mean that a lower standard of dog work will be acceptable, but only you can decide that.

To my mind there is a lot more pleasure in a wander round the outlying bits of the shoot with just the dog for company than in joining forces with fifty or so others to take part in a formal driven day. Hunting out the hedges and gutters, the little patches of gorse and bracken, the odd bits that never get beaten on a proper shoot day, will never lead to a big bag, but big bags are not the order of such a day. For a start, you will probably have to carry whatever you shoot, and a bulging gamebag weighing down your left side is not conducive to good shooting. This sort of informal, roughing in the boundaries type of day was once the prerogative of the spaniels, and a good spaniel will still take a lot of beating at this kind of work. The modern rough-shooter though has a wider choice than his forebears, since the various Hunt, Point and Retrieve breeds may also be considered. Indeed, if you have the type of mixed shoot where you may want to hunt out a hedgerow at one moment, then quarter a fifty-acre root field at the next, search a tangle of whin bushes for rabbits then try a young plantation for any woodcock that may have dropped in, a good GSP, Vizsla, Brittany or similar may be just the dog for you.

I am not a great fan of the HPR breeds when they are used solely in one of the traditional roles of the native pointing, flushing or retrieving breeds. I can see little sense in buying a dog which has the potential to do a whole range of different jobs and using it for only one, especially when there are specialist breeds available which will do that one job to a much higher standard. The handler will not, unless he is extremely fortunate with his choice of dog, have a dog which can reach the same level of excellence as one of the breeds developed specifically for that type of work, while the dog will only be worked to a fraction of its potential. Specialist work is best left to the specialists.

However, you may not want to specialise. You may want a retriever in one field, a spaniel in another and a pointer in the next. You may enjoy the challenge of training a dog which has to combine the work of all three specialist breeds. Most importantly, you may have the kind of shooting that can make use of the true potential of one of the HPR breeds. Then I would unhesitatingly recommend that you consider one. There is a lot of work in training one to meet its true potential. You will want the dog to walk quietly at heel when required yet also be able to get out and cover ground like a pointer or setter; to flush those pheasants out of the hedge bottom yet be staunch on point to the partridges in the stubble; to distinguish between live game to be pointed and dead or wounded game which should be retrieved; to work close in under one set of circumstances and run far out under another. A good HPR takes time and patience and no little skill from its trainer, but a good HPR is a treasure indeed, if you have the proper work for it. To take a free-running dog like a Vizsla or one of the German Pointer variants and expect it to spend all its time sitting by a peg, or pottering about under your feet, is asking for trouble. Not only is the dog being worked to a fraction of its potential, but it is likely to become frustrated in its sedentary role, and that frustration will find an outlet, sooner or later. Unfortunately, when it does, it is quite likely to reinforce any prejudice that your companions may have about the ability of the HPR breeds.

In the final analysis, if your dog does what you want, and does it to a standard that is satisfactory for you, then you have a good dog, at least as far as you are concerned. If you shoot alone, with just the dog for company, then you have a good dog, full stop. If, though, like most of us, your shooting is a more social affair, then you should also consider the standards of your companions before pronouncing your dog's behaviour to be satisfactory.

One badly behaved dog can nullify an awful lot of the pleasure to be gained from a day's shooting. You may be quite happy for your dog to run in when a bird falls, and there is a valid argument that the quicker the dog gets on to the scent of a runner the sooner that bird can be dispatched. Consider though the feelings of your neighbour, who may insist on his dog staying steady right to the end of the drive, if your dog has stolen all his retrieves by the time the whistle signals 'drive over'? He may well be too polite to say anything, but if you expect a proper degree of steadiness from your own dog, then it is a most annoying thing to watch an uncontrolled animal charge about and lift every bird as soon as it hits the ground. In the beating line, too, the dog which races about out of control can be a pain in the proverbial to the rest of the beaters, particularly those who require their own dogs to work within proper bounds. The sight of another dog pulling ahead, flushing game and generally having a good time is quite likely to persuade other dogs to join in and share the fun. The dogs' handlers may not see it as fun.

Some handlers seem to make a special point of never using a lead on their dogs. There are times when a lead is nothing but a nuisance, so this is fine, provided that the dog is under control. Unfortunately, it is all too often the very dogs which most need to be attached to their owners by a piece of string which are allowed free rein throughout the day. If for some reason you need to keep the dog at heel when you are walking through thick cover, then you will quickly discover just how awkward it is to lead a dog which keeps going under bramble runners and round the wrong side of trees. If you are a walking gun and want the dog by your side as you walk then you are going to have to find some appendage on which to attach the lead, since you will need both hands for shooting. If your dog has mastered the 'heel', 'sit' and 'stay' commands you can probably keep the lead in your pocket. The trouble is, lots of handlers whose dogs haven't mastered the basic commands also keep their lead in a pocket.

Top left: Working a brace of Pointers is not common these days, but here one dog delivers a grouse to hand while its running partner looks on.

Top right: Like middle distance runners, the bird-dogs carry very little weight as can be seen from the ribs and hip bones of this Irish Setter.

Above: This Hungarian Vizsla is clearly pointing on air scent as demonstrated by the high head carriage.

Above: The great advantage of bird-dogs is that they can cover much more ground than the flushing dogs. The gun is still far out of range, but the Pointer will wait for as long as it takes him to reach it.

Opposite top: English Springer Spaniel picking up behind the butts at a driven grouse shoot.

Opposite bottom: A black and white German Shorthaired Pointer retrieving a cock pheasant through rushes and birch scrub.

Top: Weimaraner pointing in rushes and bracken – the pheasant was right under the dog's nose, as evidenced by the angle of the head.

Above: A working Weimaraner: this is not a particularly wide ranging dog but it was deadly at tracking running grouse.

Below left: Kennels should be warm, dry and draught-proof, and must be secure. There is no need for a large run, though these are rather smaller than would be desirable.

Below right: English Springer Spaniel working among the heather at the tail end of the grouse season.

Bottom: The keeper and the gun discuss exactly where the bird landed as their dogs search for it in the heather.

Top: A lively English Springer Spaniel quartering across in front of a line of walking guns.

Above: One grouse to hand and the spaniel is busy looking for the next.

Opposite: This Golden Retriever has the very light coat which seems to be coming more prevalent.

Above left: Springer Spaniels and a Golden Retriever are the choice for these standing guns, though the dogs will be used as beaters in the next drive on this shoot.

Top right: Waiting and alert with one Yellow and one Chocolate Labrador.

Bottom right: Least common of the Labrador colours is the Chocolate Labrador.

You reach the end of a drive and there you are: eight guns, a dozen beaters, and twenty or so dogs. The usual postmortem is going on, the beaters are getting their instructions ready for the next drive, and the dogs are milling about. Except for one dog, which has taken itself off to do a little freelance hunting in the nearest covert, from which a steady stream of pheasants is lifting and heading for pastures new. Of course, the dog is persuaded to come back eventually, probably after a lot of shouting and whistling that disturbs the covert even more. Then, and only then, can you proceed with what remains of the next drive.

It seems to be one of Nature's laws that the dogs which are most likely to take themselves off and cause mischief are invariably owned by the handlers who take the least notice of them between drives. In practice, it is because the owners are not concentrating on the dogs that the dogs are able to slip away. What is strange though is that it is generally these same owners who are most adamant that they will not put the dog on a lead between drives. To be fair, given the opportunity and a sufficient lack of restraint, almost any gundog will be more than happy to trot off and do what comes naturally among the pheasants. Free hunting is pure pleasure, at least until the handler catches up with him again. Consider though the well trained, well behaved gundog, working with and for its handler. That dog will take just as much pleasure from its days in the field, provide a whole lot more enjoyment for its handler, and won't ruin the day for everyone else.

Working a gundog is, or should be, a pleasure for both dog and handler. True, things don't always go well, mistakes are made, dogs have off days or days when they seem to forget every lesson that they ever learned, but given time, patience, and the right sort of dog to start with there is every chance that you can eventually have a dog in which you can take a real pride. More than anything else, the end result will depend on the effort that you have put in during the training and early working period of the dog's life. There is a very real correlation between the time you put into the dog as a puppy and the pleasure you get from the dog as an adult. If you want to get the best out of your dog over the eight, ten, perhaps twelve years that you hope he will be working with you, then it must make sense to put in that little extra effort to get him 'right' during the first year or so when he is being trained and worked. Then working your dog will be a pleasure, not only to you and the dog, but to your shooting companions as well.

Field Trials

Field trials have been around in one form or another for about one hundred and thirty years, the first recorded trial taking place in Bedfordshire in 1865. The trial was only for pointers and setters, and field trials remained the exclusive property of the bird-dogs for the next thirty-four years, until 1899 when a trial for spaniels was organised, followed a year later by one which invited entries from dogs which retrieved, though the entries included a number of spaniels as well as dogs from the recognised retrieving breeds. Retriever trials proper began in 1901.

At the beginning of this century the Kennel Club took charge of all field trials, and it has maintained tight control of them ever since. All trials must be licensed by the Kennel Club and run under Kennel Club rules, all dogs which run in trials must be registered with the Kennel Club, and judges of trials must have Kennel Club approval. Anyone who contravenes these regulations risks being banned from the Club. The Kennel Club's disapproval may not sound too dire to the average shooting man who has no interest in dog shows or field trials, but it is a very serious threat to anyone who breeds, shows or trials their dogs.

It may seem unreasonable that you cannot organise an off-the-cuff field trial for dog handlers in your locality without every person, and every dog, taking part being drummed out of the Brownies, but that's the way it is. It is not an infringement of your personal liberty, in that the Kennel Club does not say that you cannot organise your own trials; it merely says that, if you do, you will no longer be welcome to take part in any of its activities, including having your pups registered. And of course, if your puppy is not registered it cannot take part in any Kennel Club show or trial.

There have been odd moves over the past few years to form a breakaway group of working gundog owners who would run a registration scheme, organise trials and generally duplicate the work of the Kennel Club without all the red tape and regulations. Though the idea has some attraction I think, on balance, it is probably better to have one Kennel Club, albeit in a monopoly position, than to have a rash of breakaway organisations springing up, since this would almost certainly result in a lowering of the standards that the Club has sought to maintain over the years. For an example, we need look no further than what has happened to standards in world championship boxing since the sport was allowed to split into half a dozen factions. Critics of the Kennel Club may consider it overly bureaucratic, but there is no denying that under the Club's guidance field trials in Britain have been maintained at a consistently high standard.

There are four different classifications of field trial: Pointer and Setter Trials, Spaniel Trials, Retriever Trials and HPR Trials. Of the four the HPR Trials are by far the most recently established, their history in Britain dating back less than forty years. The Kennel Club sets the rules and regulations for each category of trial, and also publishes detailed guides for judges which expand and clarify the rules as well as advising judges on the organisation of the day. The short-term objective of a field trial is to allow a comparative assessment to be made of a number of gundogs working under similar conditions, and to make awards to those dogs which perform best on the day. In the longer term, by encouraging comparison and competition, and rewarding excellence, it is intended that standards of gundog work can be maintained and improved, and that the best working lines may be identified for the guidance of breeders.

A field trial held under the present Kennel Club regulations is very much a competition, with the dogs being placed in an order of merit. If the two best dogs on the day have worked to an identical standard the judges must find a reason to separate them, placing one above the other. If only one dog has worked well enough to receive an award then only one award will be given, and it need not be first place if the judges do not consider that the standard of work was sufficiently high enough to deserve such an award. On the other hand, if there are ten dogs worthy of an award only four can be placed, though the rest can be given Certificates of Merit.

On the Continent there are tests organised where the dogs are judged against a standard rather than against each other, and awards are made according to how well the dog has worked rather than how well it has worked in relation to the other dogs. Spring Pointing Tests for Hunt, Point and Retrieve breeds have been organised along these lines, but the great majority of field trials continue to take the form of a competition between individual dogs.

Trials are organised in several different categories according to the age and experience of the dogs taking part. Puppy Stakes are self-explanatory, while Novice Stakes are limited to those dogs which have not won awards above a specified level. Breed Stakes limit their entries to dogs of a particular breed, and there are Open and All-Aged Stakes for the more experienced dogs. At the top of the list are the Champion Stakes, which are held annually, victory in which carries the automatic award of Field Trial Champion status. The Pointer and Setter Champion Stake is held in

Scotland and England in alternate years; there is a Retriever Champion Stake, an HPR Champion Stake, and Champion Stakes for spaniels – which in practice means Springer Spaniels – and one for Cocker Spaniels as well. Winning the Champion Stake makes up a dog to Field Trial Champion, as does winning two of the Open, Breed or All-Aged Stakes.

The organisation of field trials varies considerably between the four different classifications, though the overall aims are the same. There are generally more entrants than there are places available, a state of affairs that is unlikely to improve as interest in field trials seems to be growing, and increased leisure time and improvements in mobility make it easier for more and more gundog handlers to take up trialling.

A frequent criticism levelled at novices is that they enter dogs which are not sufficiently well trained and experienced to justify their inclusion in a trial, and by so doing exclude others who would be better able to compete. The criticism is valid, though there is a counter argument that any handler who has paid their fees should be entitled to the chance to take part. Certainly, if only experienced trial handlers were allowed to take part there would be no 'way in' to the trial circuit for the novice, and sooner or later field trials would die out, which is most certainly not a good idea.

The original trials were organised by shooting men for shooting men, and were essentially competitions between working gundogs. Since then the interest in trials has spread to many gundog owners whose involvement with gundogs is primarily as field trial competitors rather than as practical, working gundogs. Evidence of this can sometimes be seen in the relative emphasis that is placed on certain aspects of gundog work, with field trial enthusiasts looking primarily for things that the practical shooting man might consider less important than the simple basics.

Of the four field trial disciplines Pointer and Setter Trials are by far the oldest, and have enjoyed a considerable revival in popularity over the last twenty years or so. There is no requirement for game to be shot at these trials since the dogs are tested only on their game-finding ability, retrieving, as we have seen, not being considered a normal part of bird-dog work in Britain. This has had a number of effects on Pointer and Setter Trials.

The trials can be held during the close season. This was a great advantage during the early years of field trials when poor transport would have made it impossible for many of the best dogs to attend the trials during the shooting season when their services were required on the moors. The modern circuit begins with Spring Grouse Trials in the north of Scotland at the end of March, followed by Spring Trials on partridge and pheasant in East Anglia during early April. The summer Grouse Trials begin in England during July and move into Scotland during August, ending usually a day or so before shooting starts on the twelfth. Then there are Autumn Trials in East Anglia again during September, which ends the English/Scottish trial season, though in Ireland Pointer and Setter Trials carry on well into the autumn. Since no game needs to be shot the trials can continue even in a bad grouse year, when moor owners have cancelled all shooting in order to conserve their birds. Indeed, running a trial may well be beneficial by helping to break up what coveys there are and encourage the birds to spread across the moor. Some gamekeepers may regret the disturbance caused by forty or so dogs and handlers wandering about their moor, though others welcome the chance to see just how well their birds have done during the breeding season.

With no requirement for birds to be shot, Pointer and Setter Trials have attracted many handlers whose interests do not include shooting over their dogs, or working the dogs for others to shoot over. Their knowledge and experience of gundog work is thus limited to the necessarily artificial nature of field trials, and their evaluation of good gundog work depends solely on this knowledge and experience. While this is not a problem when such people attend trials as competitors, it can be a serious drawback if they graduate to judging trials as well.

The task of the judges at a trial is to find the dog which, on the day, performs best *from a shooting point of view*. The emphasis is not mine; it is laid down by the Kennel Club, and quite rightly so. A gundog is first and foremost a dog which has been bred with shooting as its prime task, and any attempt to evaluate its merits as a gundog must be approached from the practical shooting angle. And yet, I was once told – by an A Panel judge, no less – that a particular dog was '. . . certainly the best from a shooting point of view, but too plain to win a trial'.

The prime objective of a pointer or setter is to locate game and indicate its presence to the guns without flushing it. The dog's efficiency at finding game will depend on how well it quarters its beat, and on the sensitivity of its nose; its ability to point that game without disturbing it will depend on the dog's bird sense and experience, on knowing when to close its birds and when to hold off them. Pace, style, handleability and so on may then be the finer points which separate one dog from another in the awards, but they should not be the prime criteria by which trials are judged. They should not be, but on some occasions they are.

The number of dogs allowed in a Pointer and Setter Trial is far higher than in any of the other trial formats, forty or so entries being normal for an Open or All-Aged Stake. There are two judges and dogs are drawn to run as a brace, though they do not compete on a knockout basis. Both dogs from a brace may go on to the next round, both may be eliminated, or one may be eliminated while the other goes through. The judges indicate the limits of the beat to the handlers and the dogs are cast off to opposite sides, in theory crossing and re-crossing in front of the handlers as they walk forward into the beat. The Kennel Club regulations permit the beat to be up, down or across the wind, though in practice it is rare for bird-dogs to be asked to work anything but a headwind, or a very slight cheek wind – a sometimes cumbersome practice at a trial which involves much needless walking, and something that most practical shooting men would consider a pointless waste of their energy and their dog's ability. With twenty-plus brace to be assessed in the first round, each brace can only be run for a very limited time, and it is not unusual for a dog to be eliminated at its first sign of poor or sloppy work.

Certain faults are identified as eliminating faults, for which the dog must be picked up and discarded from the trial. Flushing upwind, chasing game, missing birds etc. bring immediate dismissal, while failure to back a pointing dog, poor ground treatment etc., while not carrying automatic elimination, will probably mean that the dog will be discarded when the judges decide which dogs to include in the second and subsequent rounds. There are always two rounds, sometimes three or four, until eventually the judges have agreed their order of merit.

Trials for the HPR breeds differ considerably from the Pointer and Setter Trials. The initial requirement is the same in that the dogs have to find and point game, then produce it, but there the similarity ends. The dogs run individually, not in pairs, and since game must be shot to test their retrieving ability, the trials take place during the shooting season. Entries are normally limited to a dozen dogs, and the organisation of the day is much closer to that of a normal shooting day.

The dogs are expected to cope with whatever wind direction they are given, and with only twelve dogs to judge there is a tendency for the judges to be more forgiving than the judges at Pointer and Setter Trials. In general, an HPR competitor which has not committed an eliminating fault will be asked back for a second round; at Pointer and Setter Trials it is not uncommon to be dropped after one round even though the dog has done nothing wrong. This may seem harsh, but it is often forced on the judges by the number of dogs to be seen within a limited time, and it is a fact of life that the competitors generally accept quite philosophically.

Since HPR competitors have to be steady to fall of game, and to demonstrate their ability to retrieve without damaging the game, there are obviously more faults 'available' to the dogs, and more ways to get eliminated. Hard mouth, running in to the retrieve, and failure to retrieve game can all see the end of the trial for a dog, and even if all this is negotiated satisfactorily there is the final hurdle of the water test to be overcome. At the conclusion of the trial all dogs which are in line for awards have to show their ability to make a retrieve in, or across, water, and many a 'winner' has had their day ruined at this stage.

Spaniel Trials are similar to HPR Trials in that they are essentially a shooting day, and of all the trial disciplines are probably the ones that most nearly replicate the actual work of the dogs in the shooting field. The dogs are worked in front of a line consisting of handlers, guns and judges, and are expected to hunt out and flush game for the guns, be steady to shot and fall of game, and to retrieve tenderly on command. In Spaniel Trials, as in Pointer and Setter Trials, two dogs are run at the same time, but they do not run as a brace, in that each dog has its own beat and is worked independently of the other dog. In order to receive an award a dog must have been seen by more than one judge, and must obviously have demonstrated its ability to find game, produce it for the guns and then to retrieve it. The judges look, among other things, for good ground treatment, game-finding ability, courage in facing cover and initiative in hunting and retrieving, as well as the ability of the handler to control and direct the dog as required.

Trials for spaniels can be run solely on rabbits, so they continue beyond the end of the game shooting season. Indeed prior to the arrival of myxomatosis the rabbit was the quarry at most Spaniel Trials, particularly those for Cockers. Obviously the quarry will depend largely on the venue, and could be entirely rabbits or pheasants, or perhaps a mixture of these along with woodcock, hares, snipe and even grouse or blackgame in some favoured spots. The cover may be open woodland or gorse and bracken-covered hillside, rough grassland or fields of roots, and it is a good dog indeed that can adapt to whatever quarry and terrain are offered to it.

Retriever Trials take place with either driven or walked-up game, and are naturally intended to test the retrieving ability of the dogs entered. When game is being walked-up, often in root fields, the work of the dogs may seem a little remote from that expected by the practical shooting man, in that the dogs are walked at heel rather than allowed to hunt in front of the line of guns. The situation when game is driven is obviously more familiar to the shooting man, with the dogs required to sit, quietly, and to mark each bird shot, as would be normal at a driven day. Great emphasis is placed on steadiness, and on the controllability of the dogs, and not surprisingly the retrieving work is judged much more critically than is the case in Spaniel or HPR Trials.

The proportion of gundog owners who compete in field trials to those who simply work their dogs is very small. The great majority of shooting men will never enter their dog in a trial, nor even go along to one as a spectator. What relevance then do field trials have for the gundog owner who simply wants to shoot over his dog, or take it beating or picking-up?

Ever since trials first began there have been arguments over the merits and demerits of trialling dogs as opposed to shooting dogs. The arguments have altered little in the century and a quarter since the inception of field trials, and are probably no nearer to being resolved now than they were a hundred and twenty years ago. Let us consider the view from the opposing camps.

Field trials are clearly the pinnacle of gundog work. The best dogs in the country compete in trials, the best trainers handle them. The dog which gets to the top against this opposition is likely to be a far superior worker to the average, untrained and undisciplined shooting dog, and will prove far superior when used in the field. The non-trialling handlers who put down field trials are simply jealous; if they and their dogs had the ability to compete they would do so. On the other hand, field trials bear little resemblance to a real shooting day and the dogs in them are more like circus performers than proper working gundogs. They rely far too much on their handlers and lack the real initiative which is found in proper working dogs. Overpaced and generally too hot to handle, they are fine for a few minutes but would never have the stamina to put in a proper day's work in the shooting field.

Let me say right now, before I am quoted out of context, that my own views are not represented in either of the above statements. They are merely intended to outline the views of the extremists in each case. Neither is correct; that is to say, neither is wholly correct, but there is a certain amount of truth in both viewpoints. Let us look backwards a few years and sample the opinions of some earlier writers.

Mr Teasdale-Buckell, writing in 1907, said, 'For the past forty years there have been held public field trials on game for pointers and setters. Whether these events have been worked off upon paired partridges in the spring, or contested by finding young broods of grouse just before the opening of the season, they have given breeders and sportsmen the chance of breeding by selection for pace, nose, quartering and breaking. Unfortunately they have left out stamina.' Some thirty-odd years later Colonel Hubert M. Wilson was also concerned that field trials did not test the stamina – he called it 'stoutness' – of the entrants, though he first dismissed the notion that there should be any real difference between shooting and trialling dogs:

'It is often maintained that a different standard of work and training is required in a field trial setter or pointer from that which is wanted in an ordinary day's shooting. This criticism surely is not justified, nor do results confirm it. This objection has arisen owing to the fact that at field trials pace is too often considered almost first, with the result that dogs go too fast for their noses and that in consequence much game is missed. Another cause for dispute as to the merits of field triallers as against the ordinary shooting dog is owing to the craze for almost insisting that dogs at trials must always work only upwind; complaints by handlers when they are asked to work on a sidewind or downwind are well known to all judges. The practice of always working upwind, however, entails an immense waste of time and a lot of unnecessary walking.

What, then, is the dog which one would choose as very high class in all respects? For when all is said, the sport should come in front of the dog. One seldom sees a dog that fully merits this distinction, but perhaps a fair definition would be that he must gallop and stay (there are too many of the sort that run for twenty minutes only, perhaps three times in a day's work), that he must really quarter his ground, turn to the handler's whistle, and when birds are found, remain really staunch until the guns get up. There can be no objection to wide, as distinct from wild, ranging if a dog can be trusted when birds are scarce, and perhaps one of the weak points of field trials is that they are often run on ground too full of game, which prevents the fine ranging stout dog showing what he is made of.

Some of the old records as to this question of stoutness are interesting. For instance, at Bala in 1867, the trials were run in three-hour heats, and at Vagnol in 1870 comment was made on the fact that one dog was only down for one hour, while a bitch, Ruth, ran for a full two hours. In 1873, when trials were held at Orwell in September, all dogs had to be down for at least three-quarters of an hour under the judges, Mr Shirley and Mr Lort, who were shooting. If trials were held in the shooting season and judges carried the guns, I fancy that dogs would not be forgiven for missing game as they are today.'

Colonel Wilson's remarks as to the length of time that dogs are run in Pointer and Setter Trials provide an interesting basis for comparison with the same trials today, where it would be quite exceptional for a dog to run anything near twenty minutes in the course of a day, never mind in one round. A few years ago I timed one of my own dogs which my wife was running in a novice stake. He ran in two rounds and was down under the judges for a total of just four and a half minutes, including having a find in both rounds. And he won the trial.

Logically, trials cannot test for stamina within the time limits available to them. Take a typical bird-dog stake with forty dogs entered; that is to say, twenty brace to run in the first round. Assume a nine-thirty meet, half an hour to get from the meet to the starting point for the first brace, half an hour for lunch and half an hour to get back off the hill for a finish time of five pm, which leaves six hours. Knock off a couple of hours for waiting for dogs to be called up, judges' deliberations, walking back after each upwind beat and generally getting everyone into the right place at the right time and you are left with four hours of dog work at an absolute maximum. Spread over twenty brace that allows a total working time of twelve minutes per dog.

In practice some will do much less because they are eliminated early in their run; others may do quite a bit more, but no dog is likely to run for more than half an hour in a whole day. Compare that with the 'three-hour heats' that Colonel Wilson remembered from Bala a century and more ago, but compare with caution. If they really did run their dogs in three-hour heats, then the judges would presumably have only seen two brace of dogs in a day, with an absolute maximum of three brace if they started at nine am and worked through to six pm without a break. On that basis the first round of a modern day Pointer and Setter Stake would take ten days!

And what of the dogs that could run for three hours at a stretch? A day on the hill after grouse is hard work for man and dog, and it would take a very fit party to do much more than six or seven hours' actual walking in the course of one day, allowing for the lunch break. Two dogs might cope with the work on an occasional basis, but to work regular, back to back, six-hour days I would want three dogs as a minimum; four would be more realistic. That means an average time down for each dog of one and a half to two hours, and they would be more than ready for their kennels by the end of the day.

Now I know that some handlers claim to have dogs that will work all day, six or eight hours at a stretch, with hardly a break. Remember, we are talking about pointing dogs on the hill, not non-slip retrievers. I have actually seen a couple that were supposed to possess this tremendous stamina, and to be fair they would toddle along for hours at a time, and 'toddle' is the right word. Moving at barely a trot, both of these wonder dogs would actually cover about a quarter of the ground that a good going pointing dog would have worked. Fine if you happen to be shooting on a densely stocked driving moor, but not a lot of good on a typical dogging hill with birds about as common as hens' teeth.

Spaniel and HPR trials are sometimes accused of failing to test the dogs' stamina, but here there is less cause for complaint. With only a dozen dogs to judge there is obviously more scope for giving each one a decent run, even if there is not time to really probe their staying power, and it is not unusual to read reports, particularly of Spaniel Trials, where the judges have preferred a particular dog because it stayed the course better than a rival.

HPR trials have at times attracted a lot of criticism from spectators accustomed to the standards of dog work expected in the other three trial classifications. At a bird-dog trial any transgression – sloppy ground treatment, failure to drop to flush, lack of pace – will usually mean that the offending dog is picked up and eliminated forthwith. A missed retrieve at a Retriever Trial usually signals the end of the proceedings for the offending dog. The rules are generally applied more strictly than they are written, the judges' intention being to avoid wasting time seeing dogs that will not feature in the awards. By contrast, HPR trials seem at times to be astonishingly tolerant of faults, dogs which would have been discarded in mid-run at other trials being allowed a full run, and then brought back for a second round. The first few times that I watched HPR trials I was dismayed at the time the judges appeared to 'waste' on indifferent, and sometimes downright poor, dogs. Later, one of their A Panel judges took the time to explain the reasons.

To begin with, the trial is organised alongside a shooting day; the host and the guns are entitled to expect a full day shooting over the dogs, and if they were eliminated as freely as bird-dogs, spaniels and retrievers then the trial might well be over before lunch. There are certain faults – hard mouth, running in to shot or fall, chasing fur or feather – for which the dog must be eliminated; other faults merely require that the dog is marked down. The intention, time and weather permitting, is to give all the dogs a second round, barring those which have had to be eliminated. Thus the guns get a full day's shooting, the handlers are given a good run for their money, and every dog has the chance to show that it can do good work, even if it has made a mistake early in its first run. As to the faults which would have eliminated the dog in other trial disciplines, the fact that a dog completes two rounds does not mean that it will appear in the awards, and in making their decision the judges will look at the day's work as a whole, balancing good points against bad. An early transgression may not mean the proverbial early bath, but it may well mean fourth place instead of first, or even no place at all.

I now view HPR trials in a slightly different light, and can appreciate the logic behind them. From a trialling point of view my main criticism would be that this slightly lax attitude does tend to encourage sloppy work and a lack of discipline from handlers; there is nothing which concentrates the mind more sharply than being asked to 'pick up your dog' when only thirty seconds into the run which you have travelled half-way across the country to make. From the shooting man's point of view though, and that is the objective, an HPR trial much more closely resembles a day shooting over the dogs than does a Retriever or a Pointer and Setter trial.

For most shooting men field trials are something that other people do, and their nearest connection to the trial circuit will be the dogs marked in red ink on their own dog's pedigree. What value, then, do field trials and field trial champions have for the practical shooting man?

The most obvious benefit probably lies in those red ink entries on the pedigree. That a dog has managed to achieve Field Trial Champion status may not guarantee that it will have thrown progeny that will meet your requirements in the shooting field, but it is a guarantee that that dog is bred from working stock. (Almost equally useful in some breeds are those red ink 'Show Champion' entries which mean the dog is bred from show stock and therefore should be avoided.) There are exceptions in both directions, but if you know nothing else about the breed, then the presence of field trialling blood in the pedigree gives at least a hint of the pup's likely abilities. An expert can predict a great deal about the likely – I stress 'likely' – potential of the progeny of a mating if he is familiar with the lines of the parents, and field trials give the public, expert or otherwise, the chance to see dogs in action, and to compare them with others working at the same time and under similar conditions. The fact that trials are open to the public allows the owner of a shooting dog who perhaps wants to find a sire for a litter to go along and see a number of potential sires in action, a far better idea than simply making your choice based on which dog won and which dogs were beaten.

It takes ability and training to win a trial. A well trained and expertly handled dog will probably beat a poorly trained dog every time, even though the poorly trained dog has far greater potential and ability than the winner. However good the dog, if it is unsteady or lacks the basic discipline required by the judges it is unlikely to win, but it may well be an excellent sire or dam for future generations. It is the inherent ability that is passed down in the genes, not the silver cups on the sideboard. The best dog on the day will win the trial, but it may not be the best dog in the trial, nor the best one to sire your litter.

Perhaps more important from the point of gundog work are the standards that field trials have impressed on the sport. Left to our own devices we will train our dogs to a certain level, and probably be content with the end result. Visit a few trials though and our eyes may be opened to the potential locked within our dogs. We may not want or need the dog to be trained to the same degree, nor to work at the same rate as the trialling dogs, but they do give us an idea of what can be achieved, and a benchmark to set our own performance against.

Let me give the final word to Mr C. A. Philips, writing in the Lonsdale Library publication *Hounds and Dogs*. The time is 1943, about half-way between the inception of Spaniel Trials (Philips' subject, though the sentiments apply equally to the other disciplines) and the present day. He writes:

'The advent of these trials has been of the greatest value, and importance in the advancement and progress of the spaniel breed, although there may still be a few who are somewhat sceptical of this, but their numbers grow less. In the first place, these trials have been the means of bringing those sportsmen together whose interests are centred in spaniel work and spaniel training, and largely owing to this fact we have been enabled to discover some of the best strains of working spaniels in the British Isles. We have also learnt during the last thirty years how, by judicious mating and scientific breeding, to make the best use of each strain, fostering those qualities we wish to retain, and eliminating the less desirable ones. The scientific breeder will patiently acquaint himself with the family history of the strain or strains he intends to introduce for the improvement of his own Kennel. Trials in addition have had a far-reaching effect on the show-bench spaniel, for they have corrected those absurd exaggerations that were so pronounced in these varieties some thirty years ago, and from a sportsman's point of view, have greatly improved their appearance. The reader must not infer from the foregoing remarks that field trial dogs have arrived at that state of perfection where there is little room for improvement, nor that our best dogs are greatly superior to the really good dogs that have preceded them, but the real improvement has been in the general levelling up of the rank and file. Whereas in the past some one or two stood away from the rest in point of merit, or what is termed in a class by themselves, the majority of those competing now in a strong all-aged stake are separated only a small margin. As each year passes it becomes more difficult even for the best to win a stake.'

Later he goes on as follows:

'In pre-trial days it was no uncommon sight to see even the keepers, with their dogs tethered to their sides, quite surprised when the writer entered a turnip field with his dog free and showing no inclination to run in to the fall of a bird. As a matter of fact, trials have done more for the education and training of dogs than people realise. In times past it was quite a difficult matter to find a reliable person who could thoroughly train a dog. Now they are to be found in plenty and their numbers are yearly increasing, and on account of this improvement the ordinary shooter should find no difficulty in getting a youngster broken for his own use. It has already been mentioned that trials have been the means of discovering the best strains of working spaniels in this country. From this no doubt the majority of spaniel lovers will have benefited. Therefore when we come to sum up these points the writer has enumerated, fair-minded readers will be bound to admit that field trials have been of advantage to the ordinary sportsman.'

There isn't really anything that I need to add.

General Care of the Gundog

Owning a gundog brings with it certain responsibilities. You are responsible for the welfare of the dog itself, and for the behaviour of the dog with regard to others – other people, other dogs, and other animals in general, both wild and domesticated. It is not a responsibility that should be undertaken lightly.

The dog is a predator and a pack animal, and no matter how little physical resemblance our modern breeds of dog may bear to their wolfish ancestors, deep down inside every dog that predatory pack animal is lurking still. The gundogs, bred to hunt using the instincts and inherited behaviour patterns of their ancestors, are not that far removed from their wild forebears. No matter how quiet and gentle he is when relaxing on your Axminster in front of a radiator, your dog may be an entirely different animal if it finds itself loose and unsupervised among a flock of sheep. It is up to you, as a responsible owner, to ensure that the situation doesn't arise.

A working gundog will probably spend about two per cent of its lifetime actually working, or being trained to work. Even a keeper's dog which is used regularly for beating and picking-up is unlikely to spend more than six or eight per cent of its life at work, and it will be an exceptionally busy dog. The owner has to ensure that the remaining ninety-plus per cent of the dog's time is spent in a safe, comfortable and civilised manner. The dog itself will be more than willing to spend a great deal of that ninety-odd per cent in sleeping. Humans tend to work to a regular schedule, taking our eight hours' sleep somewhere between dusk and dawn and then spending the rest of the day doing things. If there is nothing that we have to do then we tend to find something else to do, even if that something is simply sitting in front of the television and going square-eyed with boredom. In contrast, a dog with nothing to do will do nothing except curl up somewhere comfortable and sleep.

Now I know that there are those among you who will consider this as a piece of nonsense, and cite the case of the puppy which ripped up the carpets and curtains, destroyed the three-piece suite and pretty much wrecked the family home while the family was out at work. Or perhaps you will be remembering the dog which took itself off into the great outdoors and spent long, happy days hunting pheasants around the release pen, or perhaps chasing livestock on the farm. Exceptions to the rule? Not really. A dog which has nothing to do will do nothing. On the other hand, a puppy which is left alone in a room full of soft furnishing does have something to do: it has all that lovely, chewy material on which to exercise its jaws. The dog which is able to get out of the garden and into the countryside, unsupervised, is most definitely a dog which has something to do, and you will be lucky if that something doesn't result in it getting shot. Given the opportunity dogs, particularly young dogs, will find things to do if the space or the material is available, but I repeat again: the dog which has nothing to do will do nothing.

Which brings us first to the question of kennelling, or perhaps I should say 'housing' the gundog. The first question – whether the dog should be kennelled, or should live in the house – is one about which the various experts differ to a considerable degree. At one extreme there is the view that a working gundog should live in a kennel, and only in a kennel, and that allowing it access to the house and family will see it ruined in short order. Others will argue that there is no reason why a working dog should not double as a family pet. I would suggest that an awful lot will depend on what sort of family we are considering, and what role the dog is expected to play in relation to the family.

Some working gundogs are simply that, working gundogs. Those handlers such as keepers and professional dog trainers who have a considerable number of dogs in their care may keep their charges in kennels as much from necessity as from choice. There is a school of thought which maintains that a gundog should live in a kennel, and leave the kennel only for training, work or for strictly controlled exercise which is itself almost a training session. Such a regime may well produce extremely good gundogs, and quite contented gundogs too, provided that their kennelling is dry and warm and that they have sufficient food, exercise and work, but it is unlikely to suit the shooting man who wants his dog as a companion and a pet as well as a worker.

At the other end of the spectrum is the dog which lives in the house and is a family pet which goes out and does some work on shoot days. I have seen it argued by more than one professional gundog trainer and writer that it is impossible to produce a good, working gundog if the dog is allowed to live with the family. While I can see and appreciate the logic of their argument, I have seen plenty of good, and sometimes very good, working gundogs which were, to all practical purposes, family pets. Keeping the dog in a kennel may well be better and more efficient method, particularly for the professional trainer with a lot of dogs to look after, but there is no overriding rule that says you cannot keep your dog as a member of the family and still have a good working gundog.

A compromise that works well for many owners is to have kennels available to be used when required, but to have the dog in the house at times also. You may kennel the dog during the day while you are at work, and then bring it in to the house when you are at home. You may have the dog with you during the day and then kennel it at night. You may want the dog to be in the house as a burglar deterrent when you are out, but to stay in the kennel the rest of the time. Obviously, it all depends on your family, your lifestyle, and the time you have to spend on the dog.

Small children and dogs are not a particularly good mixture unless the children understand that games of tug-of-war and chase the stick are not good training for a young retriever, and are themselves well trained enough not to go ahead and play them anyway. Some dogs have the capacity to separate work from play in their minds, and will suffer no harm from playing with the children, but others can be ruined in very short order. If the dog is allowed to chase rabbits, tug at the leash, disobey commands and generally misbehave when he is out with the children there is every chance that he will think he can do the same when he is out with you.

The kennel, if you decide to have a kennel, need not be particularly elaborate provided that it is warm, dry and draught-free, and secure. If you are going to go off and leave your dog, or dogs, in a kennel, then you must be sure that they will remain in the kennel until you come back. Obviously, in this case, I am including whatever arrangement you may have made for a run in the general term 'kennel'. It pays to get this question of security right, and to get it right first time if at all possible. Dogs can be quite ingenious at digging under, climbing over or pushing through fencing, and some dogs, if they have managed to escape once, will become persistent offenders. If, though, they accept from the beginning that their quarters are escape-proof, they will soon give up trying to get out. Apart from the odd nutcase of course.

Small kennels are better than big kennels in the winter, since the dog's own body heat will help to keep it warm – and obviously, the better insulated it is the warmer it will stay. Remember, though, that you will have to be able to get into the kennel to clean it out. Very small, traditional type kennels fitted with an opening roof are easy to clean, as are the much larger, walk-in type. It is the in-between sizes, too small for you to enter but too big to clean easily from outside, which cause problems. If you happen to have a large kennel and a small establishment of dogs then an enclosed box type arrangement within the kennel can provided a warm, draught-free environment which a conventional bench would not.

The run, unless it is very large indeed, should have a concrete, stone or slab surface rather than grass, since grass will quickly become mud in the winter. A stone or concrete surface is good for the claws and feet as well as being easy to keep cleaned and washed down, and difficult for the persistent escaper to dig under. A large run is not necessary, the idea that the dog will exercise itself being generally false. Some dogs will race around in a run – puppies certainly do – but in general adults are content to wander about, watch the world go by and sleep. A raised wooden bench of some sort is popular, though it should not be raised so high as to compromise the security of the establishment. The traditional iron bars set into a low stone wall are probably the best surroundings for the run, but they are also among the more expensive. Chainlink fencing, properly strung and let into the concrete at the bottom, is a more usual compromise, but beware of the square-meshed sheep and pig netting sold by agricultural merchants. It is cheaper than chainlink, and quite strong enough to keep the dogs in, but it has one snag, as I discovered a few years ago.

We were keeping one of the pointers in a kennel with a run surrounded by a double banking of pig netting, make a six-foot-high barrier. One day the dog arrived at the front door. I returned him to the kennel, checked carefully for gaps in the fence, then went back to the house. He was there before me. I put him in again, hid behind a tree and kept watch. He simply climbed up and over the fence, just like a man going up a ladder, with front paws hooked round the wires to keep his balance. We ended up having to wire over the top of the run to keep him in. As it happened there was no problem: the dog simply came up to the house and scratched at the door with a silly grin on his face; but suppose we had been out? And living near a busy road? We are fortunate at the moment in living in a house with its own, purpose-built kennel block, complete with proper runs, drainage, lighting and water supply. Most of the dogs are primarily kennel dogs, though there are always some living in the house for reasons of youth, age, infirmity, or simply because they happen to be house dogs. If there is a difference in attitude and ability between the kennelled dogs and those which live in the house it is not so obvious as to be apparent to me. All the dogs, house dogs included, can and do spend time in the kennels when necessary, and none of them seem to object to being temporarily 'downgraded'.

Some dogs like having a bone or two about the kennel to occupy their minds and jaws, though you must take care that the bones are not the cause of trouble if you have more than one dog per kennel. Obviously there should be clean, fresh water available at all times, and if there is a standpipe and a hose handy your kennel cleaning routine will be greatly simplified.

Once you have your dog comfortably and safely housed you must give some thought to feeding the brute. This can be quite cheap, or horrendously expensive, depending on what variety of food you buy, and on whether you have access to some form of 'free' food. We managed for several years to keep a team of pointers and setters extremely fit on a diet based around boiled-up deer heads, but we were living on a stalking estate at the time. If there is a slaughterhouse nearby you can do a lot worse than feed tripes, either raw or boiled, and very well the dogs will do on them, though it helps if you have a detached, very well detached, residence and some sort of shed to house your tripe boiler. Boiling tripes have a distinctive and somewhat pungent aroma which may not be to everyone's taste.

If you have just the one dog then the cost of feeding it is not likely to be a significant drain on your budget; if you have a dozen or so then you may need an understanding bank manager. There are any number of 'complete' dog foods on the market, and the nutritionists will probably tell me that they supply everything a dog needs, and that it is a waste of money and nutrients to supplement them with meat, stock, tripe, boiled stags' heads or anything else. I wouldn't presume to argue the case from a dietary point of view, but I can say that our mob definitely prefer their all-in-one ration with a little something added for flavour, even if they don't need the extra proteins and fats.

There is no 'best' ration for a working gundog. You may like to feed tinned dog food and biscuits, raw meat and kibbled maize, cooked meat and biscuit, cooked meat and meal, all-in-one cubes, nuts or meal, leftover kitchen scraps, best fillet steak from the butcher or whatever your fancy and your pocket will run to. If the dog can maintain its body weight while doing its work, enjoys its food, and doesn't suffer from food-related halitosis, flatulence, diarrhoea or hyperactivity, then you should probably just carry on with what you are doing. The dog isn't likely to mind.

I still have a diet sheet that was given to me when I bought our first Irish Setter, something like a quarter of a century ago. It recommends a pound of meat per meal, and adds 'steak is very popular'. As far as I can remember we never actually found out whether steak would be popular with Simon, though our butcher once gave him a whole leg of lamb which he carried all the way home before he got round to eating it. Dogs were allowed into shops then, and I never heard of anyone dying as a result, though it's a hanging offence to take a dog into a food shop these days.

There are some extremely expensive dog diets on the market which will feed your dog at least as well as those costing about a quarter of the price. If you want to pay forty pounds a bag for dog food then do so by all means, and you will be able to watch little Fido munching his way through a fortune in the knowledge that you have given him the best money can buy. Alternatively, you can pay about a third of that price and still feed him just as well. It's really up to you; the chances are that the dog won't mind as long as the food comes regularly and in sufficient quantities. I am somewhat of the same mind myself.

Feeding and fitness are closely linked. It is obviously in the interests of both you and your dog that the dog is fit enough to undertake a day's work whenever you take to the shooting field together. The right diet, and not too much of it, is one of the cornerstones of fitness. Exercise is another. It is, or it certainly should be, unnecessary to say that a gundog needs to be fit in order to carry out its duties in the shooting field. How much effort you will need to make in order to get your dog to working fitness will depend largely on the breed of dog, and on the work that you want it to undertake. If shooting to you means standing at a peg while birds are driven over you, and being transported from peg to peg by Range Rover, then your dog may not need to be exactly jumping out of its skin in order to toddle out and retrieve your birds. If, on the other hand, you plan to spend the month of August tramping across several hundred square miles of the Highlands in the wake of a team of pointers, then you will probably have to spend a fair part of June and July in ensuring that those pointers are fit enough to do the job.

Dogs which are used to hunt for live game will almost certainly have to be fit if they are to do their job properly. Spaniels, pointers, setters and the HPR breeds are all expected to cover an awful lot of ground in the course of a day's work, and a dog which is not fit will simply not be able to cope. Depending on the character of the particular dog, it may simply refuse to hunt once tiredness sets in, or it may push itself so hard that an injury results. Torn ligaments, pulled muscles and skinned paws are the all too common result of asking a dog to do more than it is capable of doing. The dog will have to put up with a lot of discomfort, you may lose a few days' shooting as a result, and worst of all, the dog may even suffer a permanent injury that will affect it for the rest of its working career. If you want your dog to work properly then you should make sure that it is fit to do the job.

Exercise is the answer, and the best exercise for getting a dog fit to work is the exercise that most closely approximates to the work that the dog will be doing. Our routine for getting the pointers and setters ready for the shooting season starts way back in June with lots of long walks to harden up the pads and as much free running as is practical, bearing in mind that the game birds are nesting and raising chicks at this time. Walking, jogging or riding a bicycle with the dogs trotting alongside are all useful, though you need some very quiet roads if you are exercising a dog beside a bike these days.

Once the grouse chicks are old enough – about the second week in July – we will start taking the dogs on to the hill to carry out grouse counts. This is, to all intents, exactly what they will be doing when the shooting season starts, and is the best possible exercise. However fit they may seem after their road work, an hour or so on the hill will quickly take its toll. Given a few days though it is surprising just how quickly the dogs will run themselves into fitness, particularly if it is a good year and there are a few coveys to encourage them to hunt. The advantage of grouse counting, as opposed to waiting for the start of the season and getting the dogs fit by actually working them, is that we can take our time and start off with just an hour or so per day to begin with, and then build up gradually to full fitness. Taking unfit dogs to the hill is just asking for trouble, and if your dog pulls a muscle on the first day of the season you may have to manage without him for the first week or so. The same applies to spaniels, pointer retrievers, and to retrieving breeds which are expected to hunt live birds for their living. It is neither wise nor fair to take your dog straight from the lazy months of summer and expect him to bash through brambles for six or seven hours at a stretch with no ill effects. A little bit of forethought allied to an exercise routine will do wonders for the dog, and it might well help you too.

Strains and sore muscles are generally best cured by rest, but there are plenty of other things that will turn up to take you along to your local vet. All dogs should be vaccinated at about twelve weeks old, and then get booster shots annually thereafter. Distemper, leptospirosis, Parvo Virus and various other nasty ailments can all be avoided with a simple injection – and, incidentally, if you should happen to want to leave your dog in a boarding kennel for any reason, you will almost certainly need an up-to-date vaccination certificate before he will be accepted. The cost of inoculation is minimal compared with what it would cost to get your dog treated if it fell victim to one of the diseases, and there is no guarantee that treatment would be successful.

Your dog is likely to play host to a number of parasites from time to time, both internal and external. Worms can affect any dog, no matter how select you may be with his diet and the places where you exercise him, and gundogs are probably more susceptible than most. The fact that you are not seeing any signs of worms, or worm segments, in his droppings does not necessarily mean that he is worm-free. Treatment is as simple as adding a couple of tablets to his food, the older treatments which meant that the dog had to be starved for a day before they were administered having been replaced by more modern drugs. Worms can infect humans as well as dogs and some, notably the toxocara canis worm, can have serious consequences. It is important to keep the danger in context though: the occasional 'Shock, Horror, Killer Dog-Worms Blind Baby' stories in the tabloid press bear as little resemblance to the truth as do most tabloid outpourings. If you keep your dogs wormed regularly they should represent no danger to you or to anyone else.

Fleas, ticks and mites can all be picked up in the grass and are not a sign that your dog is dirty or diseased. There are readily available powders and sprays to deal with fleas and mites, and ticks can be simply removed by getting hold of them and pulling them out with steady, gentle pressure, ensuring that you do not leave the head and jaws stuck in the dog's skin. Clean bedding and a generous dusting of flea powder around the kennel and bed will help to prevent reinfestation, for a while. Then you have to get the sprays and the powders out and start again.

A good vet whom you know and trust is invaluable to any dog owner, and for the gundog owner it is a decided advantage if your vet is a shooting man himself and understands the particular demands that we make of our working dogs. The recent legislation on docking has caused considerable problems for some breeders, many of whom used to dock their own puppies as a matter of routine. Now your vet is only supposed to dock pups that are to be used as workers, and which might suffer as a result of being left with full tails. Some vets will dock puppies, others will not. Again, it is likely to help if your vet has a good understanding of gundog work and the need for spaniels in particular to be separated from the last few inches of their rudders.

If you are fortunate enough to own a generally healthy dog, and the dog himself manages to keep clear of injury while he is at work, your veterinary bills are likely to be little more than the cost of his vaccinations and booster shots. That is if you are fortunate. If you and your dog happen to be unlucky with illness and injury then you may find yourself looking for hundreds, even thousands, of pounds to cover the cost of the vet. It can be a nasty blow to the pocket or worse: if the cost of a major treatment is too high you may even be forced to have the dog put down rather than incur costs which you cannot hope to meet.

There are a number of insurance schemes available which will meet your non-routine veterinary bills in return for a modest monthly premium, and you might well like to consider one of these. A policy covers a particular dog, so you cannot take out a single cover and hope to get 'free' treatment for half a dozen assorted mutts. However, particularly if you have only one or two dogs, the premiums at about six or seven pounds per month per dog shouldn't be too onerous. Of course, if you have a dozen or so then you may be better off meeting the bills directly, particularly if the underwriters have got their sums right. If the idea appeals to you, you will probably find full details and an application form in your vet's surgery.

The average life expectancy for a dog is probably around ten to twelve years; the average human is supposedly good for three score and ten, which means that most of us are going to have to say goodbye to several old friends during our shooting careers. The change from baby puppy to raw beginner, from the youngster in his first season, through experienced professional to 'the old dog' takes place with increasing rapidity as we ourselves grow older. A general slowing down and increasing stiffness after a day's work starts the process; the final admission that the old boy isn't up to it any more signals the end. Strangely, it is usually only when a dog is on the fringe of retirement that you realise just how much you relied on him and how hard he will be to replace.

The question of what happens to the dog when he is too old to work is not an easy one, and it is one that cannot be answered for you, unless illness forces the issue. Some owners believe that when a dog is too old to work it is a kindness to have him put down rather than leaving him to spend the rest of his life idling in the kennel. Others say that a lifetime of hard work has earned the dog his retirement and the basket in front of the fire. There is a good argument to be advanced for either case, and you alone must decide which is right for your old dogs. I will only say that, at the time of writing, there are three eleven-year-old pointers somewhere about the establishment, and I would like to think that they will still be around for a long time to come, even if they are not now earning their keep. They earned it many times over a few years ago.

I can't remember a time when we didn't have a dog or a number of them around the house, and with one exception they were always gundogs. Now I have been mad keen on shooting ever since I was big enough to hold a gun and keep both ends off the ground at the same time, and I hope to continue shooting until age or infirmity forces me to give it up. Over the years, though, I have found a subtle change developing in my attitude to the sport.

Thirty or forty years ago I was interested in shooting as such, and a dog was just something that helped to provide the sport. Now I am much more interested in the dogs, and shooting is more of an extra activity that gives a purpose to the dog work. Given the choice, now, between taking along the gun and leaving the dog in the kennel, or taking along the dog and leaving the gun behind, it is the dog that will win every time. I suspect this is not that I am any less fond of shooting, only that I am growing more and more fond of dogs and dog work.

There are plenty of worse ways to spend your time.

Bibliography

Argue, Derry, *Pointers and Setters*, Swan Hill Press, 1994.

Clark, Atwood, *Gundogs and Their Training*, Adam & Charles Black, 1935.

Croxton Smith, A. et al, *Hounds and Dogs*, The Lonsdale Library, 1943.

Irving, Joe, *Gundogs – Their Learning Chain*, Loreburn Publications, 1983.

The Complete Book of Gundogs in Britain, ed. Tony Jackson, Barrie & Jenkins, 1974.

Hunter Pointer Retriever, ed. Tony Jackson, Ashford, 1989.

Marr, W., *Pointers and Setters*, originally published by Joe Dubb, 1963; reprinted by the Argue Sporting Agency, 1979.

Parker, Eric et al, *Shooting by Moor, Field and Shore*, The Lonsdale Library, 1929.

Petrie-Hay, Louise, *Gundogs – Their History, Breeding and Training*, The Sportsman's Press, 1987.

Ruark, Robert, *The Old Man and the Boy*, Henry Holt and Co, 1953.

'Stonehenge', *The Dog in Health and Disease*, Longmans, Green and Co, 1859.

Teasdale-Buckell, G. T., *The Complete Shot*, Methuen & Co, 1907.

Wood, Carl P., *Sporting Dogs*, DBI Books, 1985.

Index